TruthQuest™

BEYOND THE GAME

TruthQuest™

BEYOND THE GAME
LIVING OUT YOUR FAITH EVERY DAY WITH EXCELLENCE

**real
stories
from
student
athletes
to student
athletes**

KEITH COTE
STEVE KEELS, GENERAL EDITOR

BROADMAN
&HOLMAN
PUBLISHERS

NASHVILLE, TENNESSEE

10-digit ISBN: 0805430423
13-digit ISBN: 9780805430424

Published by Broadman & Holman Publishers,
Nashville, Tennessee

Dewey Decimal Classification: 248.4
Subject Headings: CHRISTIAN LIFE
                    ATHLETES—RELIGIOUS LIFE

1 2 3 4 5 6 7 8 9 10 09 08 07 06 05

THIS BOOK IS DEDICATED TO:

All student athletes who battle daily to live out your faith as you balance sports, school, family, friends, and church. My prayer is that this book encourages, sharpens, and challenges you to be the difference makers that God wants you to be.

Coach James Rexilius (1932–2003), the man who led me on the field and off, guided me into a relationship with the Lord, challenged me to love my family, inspired me to serve the church, and pushed me to be the best I could be. A man of a simple, deep faith whom I had the privilege of serving with, he worked tirelessly to serve others, spread the gospel, and build the church, impacting many lives for the Kingdom. I have been forever blessed by Coach Rexilius's example, his advice, and his friendship—he was a hero of the faith who truly fought the good fight, finished the race, and kept the faith.

CONTENTS

FOREWORD

As a twelve-year student athlete, twenty-eight-year football coach, eight-year track coach, and current president/CEO of the Fellowship of Christian Athletes, I cannot express how excited I am about the book you are about to read. We at FCA are constantly searching to find outstanding resources and tools that will assist coaches and athletes in their spiritual growth—tools that will help them to keep Christ at the center of all they do, in every aspect of their daily lives. With his book, *Beyond the Game*, Keith Cote has scored a 10! He challenges student athletes not only to live a life of excellence on and off the field but also to walk the paths of life each day growing stronger in their personal relationship with Jesus Christ, their understanding of the gospel message, and in being all that God has created them to be.

So many devotional books are written to generic audiences. The basic information is there, but it is missed by a certain group of people because it doesn't relate to them. The athlete has a different mind, a different heart, and a different emotional attitude than the nonathlete. Obviously, this is a much-needed book. Keith aptly directs student athletes and coaches in their spiritual walks and encourages them to move their "self" out of the way, departing from their egos, and to connect totally and completely with their Master Coach.

The last phrase of our FCA mission statement concerns being involved in a body of believers—the church. You can't play the team sport of football alone. It takes a team of people working together, executing offensively and defensively, in order to have success. I believe it is the same way with the athlete and the church. In this book, Keith also helps the athletes and coaches understand not only being involved in the church but also growing in the church and becoming a vital part of the body of Christ. He helps them to realize that it is more than simply saying, "I am a Christian." It is becoming a disciple of Jesus. Keith breaks it down and tells us how to put it all back together.

Devour this book. Use it over and over. Learn to walk the paths of life each day with excellence so that you can learn to become a true champion for Jesus Christ!

Dal Shealy
President/CEO
Fellowship of Christian Athletes

ACKNOWLEDGMENTS

I am indebted to many people who have made significant contributions to the development of *Beyond the Game*. These include:

Bo Boshers, executive director of Student Ministries for the Willow Creek Association—you have believed in me, mentored me, and given me the gift of vision. Much of what I do in ministry, including this book, is directly tied to you; it is a great privilege for me to serve with you in ministry.

To all the students who participated in this project, your stories and insights are the reasons for this book. Thanks for the time and effort it took to share your stories, to encourage other student athletes to grow in their walks with Christ.

Jackie Reitsma, my assistant, for your patience and organizational skills in this project—I could not have finished this project without you.

Steve Keels, the general editor of the TruthQuest™ product line—thanks for your friendship and desire to reach student athletes and expose them to the depths of God and His Word.

Mike Lueth, David Zimmerman, Brandy Ogata, and Retha Theron—thanks for all your tireless help in this project; your servant attitude brought this project to life.

The Broadman and Holman staff, especially Gary Terashita—thanks for your commitment and expertise in publishing *Beyond the Game* with excellence.

Kent Graham, Greg Wittstock, Steve Connor, Russ Graham, and all the others on the Sports Outreach team—your prayers, guidance, and support are an encouragement to me as we serve together to help the local church build effective sports ministries.

All the coaches and players from the Wheaton North football program—thanks for your undying commitment to the tradition of producing championship teams and more importantly players who are true champions beyond the game.

Jan Day, Dave Demas, Gordon Spahr, and the other members at Community Fellowship Church who are committed to building a model sports and fitness ministry in the church and for the Church.

Dave and Kara Zimmerman, Mark and Cyndi McClure, Dave and Sharon Christensen, Billy and Nancy Connor, and Mark and Lisa Beedle—all good friends—thanks for continuing to support and pray for my family and me, as we do life together.

Paul, J. R., Ken, Sandy, and Sue—thanks for sharing Coach Rex, your dad, with so many young men, allowing him to impact their hearts and lives forever, one of those being mine!

To my wonderful family: Angela, my wife and best friend; Samuel and Graham, my two sons and my buds; Madelyn and Camille, my two daughters and my princesses—your prayers and overflowing love are gifts to me that I thank God for each day. I love you with my whole heart!

BEYOND THE GAME

As an athlete today, you face more pressures than ever. You're called to excel in sport at a younger age; yet, you spend most of your day living beyond the game, in the moments of everyday life. You face more commitments at school, work, and church, and you can feel growing pressure from coaches, friends, and family. It's difficult to do everything and please everyone, and nearly impossible to do all with excellence.

With growing expectations comes a need to establish a clear plan that will guide you when the pressure mounts and you have a hard time seeing clearly. For you Christian athletes, a regular spiritual training plan—one that helps you love and follow Jesus more each day—is crucial for staying on the right path.

Physical training is a standard ingredient for your athletic success. In sports, it takes time and consistent training to be able to run a marathon, throw a football, shoot a jump shot, hit a baseball, and control the ball in soccer. You can't run a marathon without training first. No matter how hard you tried, you wouldn't be able to do it unless you had trained.

The same concept is true in your personal spiritual training. The apostle Paul in 1 Timothy 4:7–8 said, "Train yourself in godliness, for, the training of the body has a limited benefit, but godliness is beneficial in every way, since it holds promise for the present life and also for the life to come." Also, in 1 Corinthians 9:24–27, he said, "Do you not know that the runners in a stadium all race, but only one receives the prize? Run in such a way that you may win. Now everyone who competes exercises self-control in everything.

However, they do it to receive a perishable crown, but we an imperishable one. Therefore I do not run like one who runs aimlessly, or box like one who beats the air. Instead, I discipline my body and bring it under strict control, so that after preaching to others, I myself will not be disqualified."

Paul was telling you not only to try harder to be like Jesus. He was saying you need intensive, specific, and consistent spiritual training if you're serious about being a fully devoted follower of Jesus. Personal spiritual training simply means to focus on practices and principles that will help you become more like Jesus.

Whatever sport you seek to excel in, you and other athletes face similar challenges. To help you train for excellence, this devotional will address five crucial areas.

1. *You and Your Spiritual Life:* knowing God more and growing in your faith.
2. *You and Your Coach:* the challenges and rewards of interacting with your coach.
3. *You and Your Influence:* using your influence as an athlete to make a difference in peoples' lives.
4. *You and Your Relationships:* developing significant relationships with family, teammates, and friends.
5. *You and Your Church:* understanding and experiencing the importance of the local church in your life.

Our God has made you unique, so each personal spiritual training plan will be different. Don't get caught up in comparing yourself to others because that's not the measure of spiritual growth. Striving to know Christ more every day is the only helpful measurement of spiritual growth or transformation. As an athlete and Christian, you strive for excellence, but the true test of excellence is to continue to train—even through disappointment and failure, during difficult times, and under painful circumstances.

The lessons in these stories and the lessons you're learning from your own story will shape the principles and practices you pursue on a daily basis as part of your spiritual training plan. Take heart: God does not expect you to achieve spiritual excellence overnight, but He does expect you to grow and train each day!

How to Use This Devotional

Put in an hour in the gym with a personal trainer and you'll surely see beneficial results. In the same way, by spending time with God, your spiritual life will see results. This devotional will strengthen your spiritual training as you seek to understand how to excel in both your relationship with God and your life in sports.

Each of the book's five sections includes:

- Elite athlete challenge: Each section begins with a challenge to spiritual excellence from a professional athlete who has reached the top of his or her sport.
- Student stories: Student athletes like yourself share how God has worked in their lives and what they learned. Each story is followed by questions to help you reflect individually or discuss with a group how this applies to you.
- "Excellence in Action": Several devotions examine the lives of biblical people and how they responded to spiritual challenges. The lessons from these timeless stories can aid your spiritual training.

You can use this devotional for individual spiritual training or in a group setting. You don't have to start at the beginning and work your way through—find a section that interests you and start there.

Personal Devotions

This devotional can be a type of personal journal to return to at a later date to check your spiritual progress. Take your time. Reflect on the "What I Learned" section at the end of each story. Are there any parallels to your own life? Answer the "Questions for

Reflection or Discussion" after each story and after the "Excellence in Action" sections. Write notes in the spaces and margins of the pages, jot down thoughts or prayers about issues that seem to speak directly to you, reminding you about spiritual issues God may be prompting you to work on.

Group Study

The proper group setting can foster spiritual growth in a way that would be difficult to obtain on your own. Group settings have the advantage of more stories and experiences to share and learn from. They are also a source of strength, encouragement, and accountability. Your small group could choose a variety of ways to use this devotional. For example, the group could choose a student story or an "Excellence in Action" devotion to study and talk through the questions for discussion, or your group might decide to study all the biblical characters in the "Excellence in Action" sections and read the student stories as personal devotionals between the times you meet.

FCA Huddles

This devotional book was written with Fellowship of Christian Athletes "huddles"/small groups in mind. FCA has a unique and powerful mission statement: "To present to athletes and coaches, and all whom they influence, the challenge and adventure of receiving Christ as Savior and Lord, serving Him in their relationships and in the fellowship of the Church." This devotional has pulled out five areas that FCA student athletes need to focus on: themselves, their coach, their influence, their relationships, and their church. The book's five sections reflect these areas, making it a great tool for FCA huddles. Use this devotional to help your FCA student leadership explore these topics, better preparing them to understand and carry out the FCA mission to its fullest.

However you decide to use this devotional, remember that spiritual training deserves the same level (or even higher levels) of commitment and sacrifice you apply to physical training. Remember what Paul said in 1 Timothy 4:8, "for, the training of the body has a limited benefit, but godliness is beneficial in every way, since it holds promise for the present life and also for the life to come." I challenge you to give spiritual training your best! God will honor these efforts in your life and in the lives of those around you.

My prayer is that the stories and experiences shared in this book will remind you you're not alone. I pray that you will become fully devoted to God and be courageous enough to impact your world!

SECTION 1

You and Your Spiritual Life

Trust in the LORD with all your heart,
and do not rely on your own understanding;
think about Him in all your ways,
and He will guide you on the right paths.

—PROVERBS 3:5–6

KENT GRAHAM— NFL QUARTERBACK*

DEPENDING ON GOD

For me, football is an exercise in dependence on Christ. In football, I can't be in control of everything, and I have to depend on the other players as well as my own performance. My experience as a quarterback in the NFL taught me I have to lean on God; I have to know Christ and be totally dependent on Him, on the field and off. Week in and week out, my sport is an exercise in the area of dependence on God.

God showed this to me clearly in 1998 when I was with the New York Giants. I had played poorly one week against the Arizona Cardinals. While we had won, I had only a 46-percent completion rate and had almost lost the game for our team. I just wasn't performing well: nothing was going right; I was throwing poorly, and things weren't clicking.

✱ *Kent is a ten-year-plus veteran of the NFL, playing with such teams as the New York Giants, Detroit Lions, Arizona Cardinals, Pittsburgh Steelers, Washington Redskins, and Jacksonville Jaguars. Kent played college football at Notre Dame and Ohio State.*

The next week in practice, things still weren't going well. We would be going up against the Denver Broncos, on the longest winning streak in their history. Studying their defense, I became more nervous. They were so good at disguising their strategy, and I felt I would have to roll the dice every time I went to the line of scrimmage.

Before that game, I was at my weakest moment and had no confidence, which is awful for a quarterback. I felt I had no chance, but somehow I still felt God. My dad asked me how I felt.

> *Never try to live your life with God in any other way than His way. And His way means absolute devotion to Him.*
> —Oswald Chambers

I said, "I have no clue what's going to happen; I'm just going to try to be dependent on Christ." Even though I had studied my hardest and practiced my best, I felt that I was at my worst, that I had no control, that I was in chaos. I knew the only way I could be confident was by leaning on Christ.

With God, I managed to play a great game. It was as if I could feel God's presence, a peace in the midst of chaos. I was at my weakest point, but we beat the Broncos that day, and I was named the NFL Player of the Week. The Broncos went on to win the Super Bowl that year, but in that game, I learned one of the most important lessons of my life. God is able and wants to use me even at my lowest point; my motivation for playing is not to please people, not to please coaches, but rather to please God. I was able to do that in the purest form when I played that day.

For me, the key to dependence on God is to focus on knowing Him fully and to lean on Him, honoring Him through my sport and everything else I do in life. Whether on the field or off, God wants to use me. He wants me to give Him my best. In the midst of whatever chaos that life or sport might bring, He wants me to lean on Him. If I'm going to lean on Him, I have to get to know Him and fully trust that He will be with me every step of the way.

I want to challenge you to get in a deep, personal, committed relationship with God, lean on Him in all that you do, and let Him guide you. Be devoted to practicing spiritual disciplines in your life. Slow down and be still at times before God and let Him speak to you. Invest the best hours of your days discovering the depths of God; these eternal investments will prove to be the wisest choices you'll make.

> *"Your heart must not be troubled. Believe in God; believe also in Me."*
>
> —Jesus, John 14:1

Be encouraged by Joshua 1:9: "'Haven't I commanded you: be strong and courageous? Do not be afraid or discouraged, for the LORD your God is with you wherever you go.'"

DISCOVERING GOD

STACI

In my fifth volleyball season in a row, I expected to continue playing and hoped to receive a college scholarship when I graduated. But I'm not only a volleyball player; I'm a singer. I tend to get fired up on the court, and so volleyball involves a lot of yelling for me. My yelling was really causing problems with my vocal performances in school musicals.

In February of that season, I finally went to the doctor after not having a strong voice for two months straight because of yelling too much. The doctor found I had developed nodes on my vocal chords. Like any other callus, nodes can't heal without rest. Rest for me meant quitting either volleyball or music.

I knew I was capable of getting a volleyball scholarship for college. But being a part of my church worship team and being involved with drama were very important to me. I chose to stay with music, but I was miserable about losing volleyball. I cried out, "Lord, what about my future? What about college? What am I going to do?" All in one season, one of the most important things in my life was taken away. No longer could I rely on volleyball to give me the satisfaction it had up to that point. There was only one logical place for me to turn, and that was to the Lord.

The day after I quit volleyball I began to read my Bible every day. A miracle unfolded: The more I read and got to know God, the more I began to love God. God became more real and personal than I had ever imagined Him to be. The Word of God became active and alive to me, and I could see the power behind it. It seemed each time I read the Bible, I discovered more of the mysteries of God. The depth in my relationship with Him was growing daily; God had grabbed my attention.

> *For the word of God is living and effective and sharper than any two-edged sword, penetrating as far as to divide soul, spirit, joints, and marrow; it is a judge of the ideas and thoughts of the heart.*
>
> –the Apostle Paul
> Hebrews 4:12

After months of fervent prayer and seeking God, by the next July I knew I was ready to play ball again. By this time, my voice had regained its strength, and my confidence was built on a solid biblical foundation on Christ rather than on my own talent.

I wanted to play volleyball for God's glory this time instead of my own. Being able to play was a gift I fully appreciated and enjoyed because I knew it was from Him and not of me. Now, college is taken care of because I received a full-ride scholarship to play volleyball.

If I have learned one major lesson from this: in order to find true joy and satisfaction, I must find it in the Lord by getting to know Him through the Word. God created us for His glory, and He made us in such a way that when we do glorify Him, we find joy ourselves. His joy is our joy. There is solid evidence of this truth in my life. If I start slacking in my time with the Lord in His Word, life gets stressful and empty of joy. But it never fails; once I get back to intimacy with Him, He gives me strength to make it through anything that life throws. I now know that God is faithful to work things out for the good of those who love Him. Romans 8:28 says, "We know that all things work together for the good of those who love God: those who are called according to His purpose."

What I Learned

The word of God is like a mirror in that it shows us who we really are. It is like a map because it shows us where we need to go. It is like a portrait for it paints for us a picture of who God is.

—David T. Wallace

• Reading the Bible daily makes all the difference in my spiritual growth. It really helps my faith to develop and I have discovered more of who God is.

• Sometimes I don't have the time or ability to do all the things I want to do. It's hard to make choices at the time, but they usually help me grow and develop as a player and in my Christian journey.

• Drawing close to God gives me the strength I need to face life's obstacles.

Questions for Reflection or Discussion

1. Has there been a time in your life when you felt really close to God? Why do you think that was?

2. How does connecting with God on a daily basis affect your daily life? What about your sports?

3. How do you feel about reading from the Bible every day? Does it seem easy, overwhelming, or sometimes irrelevant? What would it take for you to commit to reading the Bible each day?

4. This is what the Bible says about the example you can be to those around you when you allow God's Word to direct your life: "You yourselves are our letter, written on our hearts, recognized and read by everyone, since it is plain that you are Christ's letter, produced by us, not written with ink but with the Spirit of the living God; not on stone tablets but on tablets that are hearts of flesh" (2 Cor. 3:2–3). How would your life and attitude change if you were embedded in God's Word, as Staci was?

Excellence IN ACTION
DANIEL: *Personal Training Pays Off*

Daniel 1:1–9

Daniel was a man who spent most of his life in foreign lands, serving foreign kings because his country, Judah, was taken over by these other nations. People had great expectations for Daniel. He was handpicked by the Babylonian government and placed in Babylon's top training program. Later, he was picked by the Persian government to be one among many Jewish administrators in the region. He showed great promise; therefore, these foreign kings placed heavy demands on him.

But Daniel had been handpicked by God much earlier to be a player in His empire, and God had similar high expectations for how Daniel would lead his life. Daniel was to be more a servant of God than a servant of any earthly king—Hebrew or otherwise.

Daniel had decisions to make. In some cases saying yes to his new authority meant saying no to God. Daniel, time and time again, chose to say yes to God. When offered a diet of Babylonian food that violated God's covenant with Israel, Daniel chose to stay true to God. When tempted to claim special powers of interpreting dreams in order to get ahead, Daniel chose to give glory to God instead. When everyone around him worshipped the Persian king, Daniel maintained his habit of worshipping, praying to, and listening to the one true God—even under threat of death.

While others tried to gain the approval of a foreign government, Daniel applied himself to the everyday practice of following God. Through his hard work and God's blessing, Daniel surpassed all his peers and became a key player in these foreign governments. While others excelled at conformity, Daniel excelled at doing the right thing. Daniel trained himself for righteousness, and his training paid off for him and all those around him. Daniel was a man who honored God with all he did. Daniel stayed true to God's training plan for righteousness, even though he was in an environment that did not even acknowledge the one true God.

Questions for Reflection or Discussion

1. Daniel was handpicked by God and so were you. How does it feel to have been handpicked by God?

2. Daniel had many challenges in his relationship with God. What are some of your biggest challenges as you try to follow God?

3. What distracts you from following God and staying on His training plan for you?

STARTING IN THE RIGHT SPOT

AARON

I was intrigued by pole vaulting and always thought that it would be a great thing to try. When I went to my school's track coach and told him I wanted to be a vaulter, he asked me how long I had been pole vaulting. I knew many of the team members had been vaulting for years, and I had to admit I had no experience. When I told him I had never tried vaulting before, I could tell he was hesitant about giving me a shot. I assured him I would give it my full effort, and so my training began.

For weeks I did nothing but run and work on jumping patterns. Then the day came when I was given my first pole. I stood against a wall and practiced how to hold it, how to run with it, and how to position it before the jump. I was training indoors, far from the pit, for most of the preseason. After a lot of work, I finally moved from the gym to the track.

> Our task is to do whatever enables us to catch the (Spirit's) wind. . . . We can open ourselves to transformation through certain practices, but we cannot engineer it. We can take no credit for this.
>
> –John Ortberg

At the end of the runway stood two bars with pegs at different levels that held the standard (a third horizontal bar that would measure the height of a jump). Before my first jump, the coach removed the standard and instructed me to run. I had to get used to the feel of the path under my feet before concentrating on the obstacle. I ran the runway, jumped successfully, and started over.

After weeks of training like that, I noticed one day that the coach had returned the standard. However, instead of being at the regulation height, he had set it at five feet. Even knowing that other vaulters could easily clear this, I found the five-foot standard intimidating. I got discouraged as I looked across the track to the high-jump pit where jumpers were clearing six feet without the aid of a pole. This even became a joke during practice: "You know, Aaron, if you let go of the pole, you may be able to jump higher." My coach had to remind me I was on a different playing field and had a different standard to live up to, and in time I would go far beyond where the others were going.

During those days of training, I never could have guessed how much they reflected my Christian walk and the pressures of the world around me. God taught me many lessons through this experience.

We're constantly put into situations that would be easier to handle if we didn't have to hold on to Christ and the standard He has set before us. It can sometimes feel as though the world is progressing faster and achieving more then we are—with less effort.

Some people in our lives even try to tell us to let go of Christ and see how much easier it would be without Him.

But we have a standard set before us not by man but by God, and it's achievable only with the aid of Christ. No high jumper will ever jump fourteen feet as a pole-vaulter will. Why? High jumpers have no pole, nothing to launch them beyond their own abilities. Those without Christ may reach a height faster than I do, but their progress is limited by their lack of relationship with Christ. The standard we Christians are to live up to is beyond the comprehension of many who cannot see it or understand it.

> *God uses ordinary people who are obedient to him to do extraordinary things.*
> —John Maxwell

I also learned it's important to start in the spot that's right for me. Because I had never tried pole vaulting before, I had to start at the beginning. If I had lied to my coach and told him that I had experience, I probably would have really hurt myself. It's the same in a personal walk with Christ: We need to start where we truly are, not where we think we should be or where others want us to be. If we try to be the people others want us to be and to live up to their standards, we can often end up frustrated and discouraged. God wants us to be ourselves, to come as we are and start our relationship with Him there. He loves us unconditionally and will walk beside us as we grow toward becoming the people He intends us to be.

What I Learned

- I need to be honest about where I'm starting from—and move forward from there.
- As a Christian, I'm held to different standards than others, so it doesn't help to compare myself to them.
- While it may seem I have to work harder as a Christian or make tougher choices, I know that God will honor my efforts.

Questions for Reflection or Discussion

1. Describe a time you tried to be someone you were not. Did
   you act as if you were better at something than you really were?
   In the end, did misleading those around you get you ahead or
   push you farther behind?

2. God clearly loves you, just as you are. He also loves you so
   much that He wants to help you become the person He knows
   you can be. What holds you back from coming to God as you
   really are?

3. How do you set your standards and values in life? Do you feel
   as if your parents set a good example? Do your friends reflect
   your values? How do you incorporate God's standards in your
   day-to-day life?

Excellence IN ACTION
DANIEL: *Who's Calling the Shots?*

**Daniel
1:8–20**

Nebuchadnezzar, king of Babylon, had brought
all of Judah's most promising young people into
his court, including Daniel, to serve him and
increase his power over the region. He wanted
to break their connection to their homeland and make them into
Babylonians. This methodical process included every aspect of
their lives, down to their diet. He ordered his new subjects to eat
the food of Babylonian kings, which was rich, high-calorie, and
fattening.

But food was a crucial aspect of God's covenant (training plan)
with His people. There were certain kinds of food a Hebrew was

never supposed to eat. Daniel and his friends knew what those foods were, and they knew that to say yes to those foods meant saying no to their identity as the people of God. So the first stage of Daniel's training in Babylonian customs became the first spiritual test of Daniel's personal training in godliness: Would he do whatever the crowd did, whatever the ruling authorities told him to do, or would he do what he had committed himself to do before God? Would he eat to fit in and move up or eat to stay faithful, trusting and depending on God?

Daniel's diet was not the issue; what was at stake was who would call the shots for him—an earthly king or the God of the universe. Daniel and his friends trusted God, and God raised them up to be chosen by the king to hold key roles in the Babylonian court.

Questions for Reflection or Discussion

1. Most rules in a family, in a school, or on a team are in place to protect people, but some people use their power to make rules that protect or increase their own power. If you were subjected to a rule that was against what you knew to be right, how would you respond?

2. Based on your personal training for godliness, do you know some of the things that would distort your training plan? How would you react if you were asked to do them?

3. This story had a happy ending: Daniel impressed his new leaders and rose to a position of authority in Babylon. Daniel chose to obey God, and God protected Daniel in this story. In what ways were trusting and following God Daniel's best option? In what ways are trusting and following God your best option as you relate to people around you?

GOD'S PLAN

MADELYN

During my senior year of high school, I flew to the University of Arizona to audition for its dance team. I had already auditioned at four other colleges and had not really been happy with their dance departments. I went to each, wanting to be swept off my feet with the feeling that this was exactly where God wanted me to be; so far, none of the schools had done it for me. It seemed all my friends had found their colleges, found their places, and knew what they wanted to study.

> Anxiety does not empty tomorrow of its sorrows but only empties today of its strength.
>
> —C. H. Spurgeon

To my amazement, I fell in love with this school. I loved the campus, the people. I felt at home there. The best part was that I loved the dance department. This was the school I wanted to attend, and I felt I was a perfect candidate.

On the day of the audition, I was ready to go. I went in with a clear head and felt confident with my dancing. The audition went great; I was on, and my dancing had never been better. I believed that I stood out among the fifty others. I felt this was it, the end of my long road. I knew I had already been accepted by the school and just had to wait two weeks to hear if I was accepted into the dance program.

Finally the envelope came. I ran to my room and prayed, and then opened the letter. I didn't get into the program. I felt that my last hope, my last everything, was gone. I had no idea what I was going to say to my parents or my friends at school when they asked me how it went. I had put all of my trust and hope in God, and I felt He had forgotten me.

I was depressed for months and angry with God. I felt I had been doing all these great things in my student ministry, that I had served God in every way He had wanted me to, and He had forgotten to make a place for me. I didn't want to go to church or even talk to God. All I wanted to do was yell at Him.

Trust the past to God's mercy, the present to God's love, and the future to God's providence.

—Augustine

It has been more than a year, and sometimes I still feel hurt and blame God. But because I went through this pain and hurt, my faith has become more real and honest. I am no longer the all-star Christian at my church, and because of that I learned to relate to God—just Him and me—and not through the things I was doing for Him. Maybe God wants something for me that's different from what I want, and maybe He knows me better than I think He does. It still is hard sometimes, hearing my friends talk about college, but I'm learning that God has me in this place for a reason.

What I Learned

- Being the "perfect" Christian and working hard doesn't mean that everything will turn out how I want it to. God doesn't give me things based on what I do for Him.
- My relationship with God needs to be grounded in Him and me, not in what role I play in my student ministry.
- God does have a plan for me—even though I can't see or understand it right now.

Questions for Reflection or Discussion

1. Have you ever felt God let you down? How did you react in this situation?
2. If you were fully honest with God about your anger, what would you say? Do you feel it's OK to be angry with God?

3. Even if you feel you didn't get what you had been hoping for
    in this situation, what part do you think God has in your
    future? How long did it take you to get over your hurt?

    • Read Psalm 42. You can see how the psalmist was strug-
       gling with the same things Madelyn was. It's OK for you
       to get frustrated sometimes too! God wants to hear you
       and will listen, even if you're angry.

    • Sit down this week and write an honest letter to God.
       Explain why you're hurt and frustrated and try to allow
       yourself the freedom to be truthful with God about the
       way you feel.

Excellence IN ACTION
DANIEL: *Big Dreams, Bigger God*

Daniel 2

Daniel served as an adviser to King
Nebuchadnezzar. He was an intimidating king,
given to using strong language and making rash
decisions. His paranoid behavior made it nearly
impossible to serve him consistently with success. One time he
demanded that his advisers read his mind and interpret his
dream—if they got it right, they would gain unbelievable power
and wealth, but if they got it wrong, they would suffer a painful
death. His advisers told the king the truth: "What the king asks is
too difficult. No one can reveal it to the king except the gods." This
wasn't good enough for the king: Nebuchadnezzar ordered that all
of his advisers be killed.

But Daniel turned to God with the king's unusual request, and
in this moment of crisis God provided deliverance for Daniel and

all the king's advisers by revealing and interpreting the dream for
Daniel.

Daniel played an important part in this episode, but it was
only a part. The advisers had been right all along: only God could
meet the king's demand, and God did so through Daniel. Daniel
could have grabbed all the glory for himself and claimed special
powers of mind reading and dream interpretation. He could have
set himself up for a life of comfort and power. But Daniel saw
that he and the king were both part of God's plan; God gave the
dream to Nebuchadnezzar and the interpretation to Daniel, and
between the two of them God's plan moved forward. This was
God's plan and His victory, and once again Daniel told the king
the truth.

"No wise man, enchanter, magician, or diviner can explain to
the king the mystery he has asked about," Daniel said. "But there
is a God in heaven who reveals mysteries." And Nebuchadnezzar
agreed: "Surely your God is the God of gods and the Lord of kings
and a revealer of mysteries." The king and Daniel played a part in
God's plan, but the ultimate victory went to God.

Questions for Reflection or Discussion

1. How do you think Daniel felt when he was asked to do the
   impossible?
2. When you're asked to do what seems impossible, how quickly
   do you turn to God? What can keep you from turning to Him
   right away?
3. How is your relationship with God affected by knowing that
   He is able to do the impossible?
4. Are there any impossible situations you're facing right now that
   you need to trust and talk to God about? If yes, take time now
   and talk to Him about it.

DRAWING NEAR

COLIN

I began to play basketball when I was very young. I've played other sports over the years, but basketball has always been where my heart is. Because I really took basketball seriously, I played not only on my school's team but also on traveling teams throughout the year.

During the summer before my senior year, I was playing in a traveling league that was really exciting. I enjoyed traveling and was getting excited about starting as a senior. I had worked hard over the years, and my efforts were beginning to pan out. Little did I know what the summer would have in store.

> *Draw near to God,*
> *and He will draw*
> *near to you.*
> —James 4:8

Our team had gone out of town for a four-game weekend tournament. In the first game I went down hard, and something happened to my knee. I was pretty frustrated the rest of the weekend, not being able to play, just watching the games. I didn't think it was serious; I still had my plans in mind, and I knew I would be a key player my senior year.

When I got home, my knee still hurt. My parents set up an appointment with a doctor to find out exactly what was wrong. I began to get pretty nervous, but I still had a few months before the season started, so I figured it would all work out fine. God had given me talents as a basketball player for a reason, and He wouldn't take that away now.

After I saw the doctor, I was told I had torn my anterior cruciate ligament (ACL) and cartilage, and stretched and twisted my medial collateral ligament (MCL). I had to have surgery immediately. I was a wreck. I really thought that I wouldn't have a chance to play my senior year. I couldn't understand why God would do this to me; I was mad and frustrated. I had worked hard over the past year to be my best, and suddenly I felt that God had taken all of that away. After years of practices and planning, my hopes seemed to disappear. Instead of the great summer I had planned, I now had months of physical therapy ahead of me.

After a few weeks of physical therapy and not being able to play, I was miserable. I decided that I couldn't go on for months feeling like this, so I asked God to keep me strong and help me develop a deeper relationship with Him. I watched my team play without me. I prayed that I wouldn't be so depressed that I couldn't play, but rather that I would encourage my teammates and keep on fighting to recover.

> *It is amazing how clear things become when we are still before Him, not complaining, not insisting on quick answers, only seeking to hear His word in stillness, and to see things in His light. Few are willing to receive that sort of reply.*
>
> —Elisabeth Elliot

A verse that meant a lot to me during this time is James 4:8: "Draw near to God, and He will draw near to you." When I finally surrendered my plans into God's hands, I sensed Him drawing close to me through this experience. Even when I would get mad, frustrated, and sometimes even bitter at myself and Him, God was there with me the whole time. I was surprised at the peace I felt even in the midst of the pain.

God blessed me with athletic talents and also watched over me in sports for many years. Even though I hurt my knee and my plans had to change, I was able to heal and recover in time to play for part of my last season. God put doctors and physical therapists in my life who helped me heal physically. Most importantly, He gave me the needed time off from my sport and the spiritual opportunity to draw near to Him. During this time, I learned to surrender myself to His plans and direction in my life and to rely on Him for courage, strength, and direction. His plans for me became clearer, and God became more real and visible to me than ever before.

What I Learned

- It helped to focus on drawing near to God when I was trying to recover.
- It's normal to feel frustrated and angry with God when you're injured. That process helped me grow and understand God more—I wasn't a bad Christian because I was upset.
- By surrendering myself to God's plan for my life, I can have peace knowing He is in control and He has my best interests at heart.

Questions for Reflection or Discussion

1. Read James 4:8 again. Do you feel that God is near right now in your life? What would it take for you to draw near to Him?
2. Can you recall a time when God's plans for you weren't the plans you had in mind? How did you feel? Was it hard to trust God through that?
3. What is the current source of your courage and strength to face life's challenges? What would it take for you to begin to rely on God for those things?

Excellence IN ACTION
DANIEL: *Just Do It, God's Way*

| Daniel 6:1–11 |

The phrase "Just do it" is meant to motivate us to follow our dreams and achieve our goals. Sometimes those goals are good ones and other times they aren't. Similarly, some rules are good and others aren't. We often hear the phrase "Rules are meant to be broken." It's mostly used as an excuse to do something we want to, regardless of whether we should. But some rules are not only annoying or inconvenient: they're offensive to God and unbiblical. Any rule that goes against the Word of God and asks us to do the same is wrong. Breaking those types of rules is the right thing to do, and God trains us to do the right thing.

Daniel faced rules he knew were unacceptable to God. Once, late in Daniel's life—after the Persians had taken over the Babylonian Empire—his new king, Darius, was tricked into making an unjust rule. The king's staff, jealous of his trust in Daniel, played on the king's vanity and desire to secure his authority in the region. They convinced the king to draft a rule that Daniel would never be able to follow in good conscience: For thirty days no prayer or worship could be offered to any god except Darius. Anyone who broke this rule would be thrown into the lions' den.

Darius knew he was not God and so did his staff. However, Darius agreed to the law for the same reason we might: We like power, and we like to be treated by others as though we are gods. It's a common human temptation, one that God goes to great lengths to protect us against.

So part of God's training program for us and for Daniel is to get us out of the habit of worshipping other people, other things, or ourselves and into the habit of worshipping Him alone. The first of the Ten Commandments that launched God's training program for the Jewish people sets this standard: "I am the LORD your God, . . . Do not have other gods besides Me. . . . You must not bow down to them or worship them" (Exod. 20:2–5). The rest of God's training program flows from this simple but fundamental concept. Daniel knew this; he knew that if he worshipped Darius, even if only for a month, he would be giving up the way of life that had helped him remain an active and effective player on God's team. He knew the only training that would improve his ability to worship and serve God alone would be difficult and sometimes painful. So

Daniel pursued his spiritual training, and therefore violated a man-made rule he could never obey. By violating this rule, he faced consequences he could never survive on his own.

Questions for Reflection or Discussion

1. What do you think Daniel felt when everyone around him was saying, "Just do it"?
2. Describe a time you've been asked to do something you couldn't do in good conscience. How did you feel? How did you respond?
3. What are some of the hardest consequences of doing the right thing? What are some of the best results of doing the right thing?

SPIRITUAL DISCIPLINES

ANGELA

Often in my life, God uses everyday things to teach me about my relationship with Him. My time competing in track and field taught me not only about physical discipline but spiritual discipline as well. I used to really struggle with my spiritual life. I thought I was always doing the same old things and not moving anywhere. I didn't feel God's presence and had a difficult time prioritizing church and devotional time. Even though I read such verses as Hebrews 12:1 about throwing off "every weight and the sin that so easily ensnares us" so I could "run with endurance," I felt I didn't have what it

> Spiritual transformation cannot be orchestrated or controlled, but neither is it a random venture. . . . We need a plan for transformation.
>
> –John Ortberg

took. I was missing something. But God slowly began using the things I was learning in track to teach me the discipline I needed to develop my relationship with Him.

To do well in my races, I must practice so I can perform to my full potential. When I'm not looking forward to training, the thought of the actual race motivates me to persevere. Being a sprinter, any type of endurance workout is draining, nearly impossible. When I'm doing endurance training, I usually want to quit. I'm not good at it, I don't feel comfortable doing it, and it sometimes seems like a waste of my time. I sometimes think I should do only what I do best—run the sprints and work on my starts and my explosiveness.

> *To take up the cross of Christ is not great action done once for all; it consists in the continual practice of small duties which are distasteful to us.*
>
> —J. H. Newman

At one particular practice the track team was running three-hundred-meter circuits, and the practice seemed endless. I wanted to give up this painful experience. The only thought that revived my motivation was the thought of the actual race: two hundred meters of unleashed intensity. That track season, I began to see development and growth that resulted from discipline in training—training not only in what I do well but also in the areas that are hard for me. I ran the best I ever had that season!

God taught me that I also needed to be disciplined about my spiritual growth. I saw that if I committed to attending church and my small group, my community and faith really did grow. When I worked hard at praying consistently and trusting God, I began to feel His presence more. When I read His Word and meditated on it more, I discovered in a deeper way who He is.

I had always thought that spiritual growth was just something that happened with time and age, but my experience with track showed me that knowing God more came mostly through my own effort and devotion to discover Him. I had been feeling spiritually out of shape for a long time, but with spiritual practice and commitment, I now feel ready to run the races God sets before me.

What I Learned

- I have to work hard if I want to succeed in sports. In the same way, a growing relationship with God also takes practice and commitment.
- Visualizing the goal ahead can really get me excited about the work at hand. By wanting to be close to God and imagining that relationship, I was able to motivate myself to put in the effort to reach my spiritual goals.
- Sometimes I have to practice in the areas that are not the easiest for me. In my spiritual life that means I need to put more effort into the spiritual disciplines that are hard for me, not just the ones that come naturally.

Questions for Reflection or Discussion

1. Read Philippians 3:13–14: "Reaching forward to what is ahead, I pursue as my goal the prize promised by God's heavenly call in Christ Jesus." What goals are you working toward right now in your athletics? In your spiritual life?
2. Do you ever feel "spiritually out of shape"? What kind of conditioning do you need to commit to in order to develop a healthy faith?
3. What kind of spiritual training comes easy for you? What is harder for you?
4. Think about mature Christians you admire. What does their passion for God inspire in you?

Excellence IN ACTION

DANIEL: *Trusting the Trainer*

Daniel 6:11–23

After Daniel violated King Darius's rule, he faced the consequence, which was being placed in the lions' den. Ancient kings kept lions' dens as a place of punishment for people who violated their laws. The lions were kept hungry so that they would eagerly maul any person thrown to them. Being sent to the lions' den was a death sentence.

King Darius knew this, and once Daniel was accused of violating his law, Darius realized that he had been tricked by his staff. Daniel was the most valuable player on his team, and he knew that Daniel had never done anything that deserved punishment. So Darius spent the day trying to get around the foolish rule he had made, to save Daniel from death.

But Darius couldn't do it. He was beaten at his own game by his own rules; according to his people's constitution, no law in his kingdom could be repealed. Even though Darius had been treated like a god for thirty days, Darius still had no power over Daniel's life or death.

So Daniel was thrown into the lions' den, and Darius suffered mental anguish. He thought he had lost his most valuable team member and had betrayed his innocent friend. But we shouldn't feel too sorry for Darius—Daniel was the one in the pit. The only thing left for either of them was hope. The night in the lions' den was a test, not of Darius's authority or Daniel's training but of God's ability to protect His players and their trust in Him to do so.

Darius had proved he was not a god worth worshipping. Would Daniel's God prove different?

"At the first light of dawn the king got up and hurried to the lions' den. When he reached the den, he cried out in anguish to Daniel. 'Daniel, servant of the living God,' the king said, 'has your God whom you serve continually been able to rescue you from the lions?' Then Daniel spoke . . . 'My God sent his angel, and he shut the mouths of the lions.' . . . So Daniel was taken out of the den, uninjured, for he trusted in his God" (vv. 19–23).

God had passed the test. And Daniel learned firsthand what God's players always learn in time: He could trust his training because he could trust his Trainer. God had Daniel's best interests at heart, and He helped when nobody else could.

Questions for Reflection or Discussion

1. What do you think was going through Daniel's mind as he was thrown into the lions' den?
2. What man-made gods compete with the living God for your worship?
3. When is it hardest for you to trust God? When has God surprised you by His ability to come through for you?
4. How does it feel to know that God is protecting you? How does that affect your relationship with Him?

SECTION 2

You and Your Coach

STEVE THONN*

A COACH'S PERSPECTIVE

I have seen the game of football as a player and as a coach. My experiences have given me a unique perspective on the relationship between a player and the coach.

I was extremely fortunate during my years as a high school and college football player to have solid coaches who were dedicated Christians. Those coaches had a huge impact on me and my life. I believe God put them in my life to guide me and prepare me for what I encounter now as a Christian coach. These coaches were very open about their faith and taught me a lot of things. I will never forget learning that I must give my best at all times in practice, in games, and in life, even if the coach or my teammates weren't watching me. These coaches really cared about me as an individual; the relationships extended beyond football into other

---

* *Steve Thonn has sixteen years of experience in the Arena Football League—first as a player for six seasons and then as a coach for ten more. Steve played with the Chicago Bruisers and the Albany Firebirds. During his coaching career Steve worked with the Firebirds, the Connecticut Coyotes, the Milwaukee Mustangs, the Houston ThunderBears, and the Dallas Desperados. He is currently with the Georgia Force. His offensive units have led the AFL four times. Steve played football, basketball, and baseball in college, where he earned all-American honors in football.*

areas of my life. I was comfortable talking and sharing with them about my struggles and asking them for advice.

When I began playing professional football, I was shocked at the huge difference in my interactions with coaches. My high school and college coaches were focused a lot more on the players as individuals. Although my pro coaches were high caliber, the focus on and interest in me as an individual were gone. My coaches on the pro level had to continue winning games to keep their jobs and, therefore, needed me as a player to help win those games. I couldn't just walk up and talk to them about personal issues in my life. The relationships were strained, and playing professionally felt more like a job than a sport.

This was very apparent to me during my first year in the pros. In one particular game I knew I was on the bubble. Some guys were going to be cut, and I was potentially one of them. I didn't know what to do in that situation because I didn't have the kind of relationship I had had with my previous coaches. I couldn't talk with the coach about my standing on the team. The disconnect between the coach and me was frustrating. After many hours of wondering and worrying, I made it past that cut. But the pressure was always there. I would see a teammate one day, and then the next day he would be gone because he'd been cut. I was always wondering, "Could I be next?" I didn't have a relationship with my current coach so I was on my own and had to completely rely on God to guide and direct me. I learned that those years in high school and college had prepared me to be, to my new coaches and teammates, an example of a player authentically trying to live each day for Christ.

Now that I'm a coach, the primary thing I try to do is be open, fair, and honest with my players. Even though coaching is my job, I want to create a positive working relationship with them. I want to be open with them and make sure they know what their standing on the team is so they don't always have to be wondering. As a coach, I know I make mistakes on the field and off. I also realize I'm not perfect. No coach is, and I don't expect the athletes that I coach to be either. I want to continue to grow as a coach and a Christian and encourage my players to grow too. I try to make sure players know they can talk to me, that I will care for them as a person and not only as a player.

> *. . . about everything. Set an example of good works yourself, with integrity and dignity in your teaching.*
> —Titus 2:7

Most situations you might find yourself in as an athlete with your coach, whether positive or negative, are opportunities filled with potential. God has allowed you to be in these situations for a reason. Even if you feel alone now, be confident that He can use these situations to develop you and influence other teammates and even your coach for eternity. I challenge you as a Christian athlete to pursue three personal goals that will set you on a path to have a lasting impact on teammates and coaches for the Kingdom.

1. *Be an example.* In all situations set a good example. It doesn't matter if you are with Christians or non-Christians. Coaches are often not interested in what you're saying. They're looking beyond this and watching your actions first. They want to see if what you're doing communicates the same thing as what you're saying. Earn your coaches' respect and ear by allowing your actions to show the same message as your words. First Timothy 4:12 says, "No one should despise your youth; instead, you should be an example to the believers in speech, in conduct, in love, in faith, in purity."

2. *Don't compromise.* Stick to your guns and don't compromise on what you believe. You need to be confident in knowing what your beliefs are and then stand firm in them. Even though it may seem OK at the moment to

give in a little bit because of pressure from teammates or coaches, it will never be worth it in the long run. Also, be ready and willing to confront your coaches with humility and respect if you know they are wrong. First Corinthians 16:13 says, "Be alert, stand firm in the faith, be brave and strong."

3. *Build relationships.* Make an intentional effort to build authentic relationships with your teammates and coaches. Although your coaches may be distant, authentic relationships will open opportunities to speak deeply about life and faith, and life change can happen. These long-lasting relationships with teammates and coaches, who you have gone to battle with, will greatly benefit you in many ways, long after you're done playing. "Iron sharpens iron, and one man sharpens another" (Prov. 27:17).

ACCEPTING MY ROLE

MAX

Halfway through the season, my baseball team was ranked close to first place. I had led in team batting average for most of the season, and it was a really exciting time to be a part of the team. Although I felt I was really playing well, my coach was having me bat close to last in the order. This really frustrated me, but I continued to strive to impress my coach and convince him to move me up in the batting order. I kept hitting better and better. Over the span of two or three games, I even had two extra-base hits. But my coach would not move me up.

I didn't understand what he was doing, and I was getting pretty upset about the situation. I knew I couldn't do much better than I was already doing, and the coach seemed to ignore my hitting. I was mad and felt bitterness toward my coach. I wasn't sure if it would even help to talk to the coach or other players. Because I was so frustrated, I started to play with a bad attitude.

Most of us are more experienced at receiving sacrifices than at making them.

–Frederick Buechner

After a few games, I started to feel convicted that my poor attitude wasn't right and realized that it wasn't going to make my coach notice my hitting abilities. If anything, it was just going to make him think I wasn't a team player. So I decided to talk to God. I told Him I needed His help to keep my attitude right and to help me accept my role that season. I decided I needed to continue hitting my best and not worry about my place in the batting order. Sometimes it was hard to hold back my pride and sometimes I wanted to give up. But, with God's help, I was able to keep a good attitude and accept my role.

God gave me some encouraging opportunities as a result. I still batted in the lower part of the order, but I got a chance to play third base more often, which I really liked. I had been playing solid defense at second base during this time, but our third baseman had been struggling. So Coach tried me out at the third-base slot and things went really well. As a result, I played third base for most of the remainder of the season and had a great time doing it.

I know that playing third wasn't some magical thing that happened because I had committed to having a good attitude. But I do know that God cares for me and wants to give me the desires of my heart. He wants me to be happy. I had really wanted to move up in the batting order, but God gave me something else that brought me joy too. He had blessed me in a way I hadn't imagined. This experience helped me see I needed to accept the role that my coach had put me in. By changing my attitude, I learned to trust and respect my coach. Even though things didn't go according to my plans, I grew a lot that year as a player and saw that God's way for me is best.

What I Learned

- God wants the best for me, and He knows what that is!
- God desires that I respect my coach even if I feel I'm being treated unfairly. My coach may have plans for me that will make me a better player in the long run even if those plans were not what I had in mind.
- God knows the desires of our hearts. He also knows what's best for us. Sometimes what we end up getting may not be what we initially wanted, but in the end, we'll see that what God provided is even better.

Questions for Reflection or Discussion

1. Do you ever feel your coach treats you unfairly? How do you usually respond? What would it take for you to have the right attitude?

2. When you feel you aren't in the role you want to play, how can you honor God in your position?
   - Perhaps you do need to work harder to prove yourself. Or maybe God is calling you to be more humble and serve your team through this role.
   - When you're frustrated about your position on the team, ask God to show you His desire for you.

3. Can you recall a time when God didn't give you what you wanted, but actually gave you something better? Thank God for providing for you.

Excellence IN ACTION
SAMUEL: *Coached in the Ways of God*

**1 Samuel
1:1–2:11**
Samuel was dedicated from birth to be a student of God's ways. His mother couldn't have children, so she made a commitment to God that if He gave her a child, she would dedicate the first child to serve the Lord all of his life. And that's what Samuel did.

At a very young age Samuel was brought to live with, work under, and be taught by Eli, the priest of the tabernacle. Eli welcomed him into the tabernacle community and coached him in a life of serving God.

Samuel saw the good and bad sides of his coach. He saw how amazing it was to learn about God and be coached by someone who had spent many years serving God. He also saw a few among the tabernacle community—Eli's sons—use their positions at the tabernacle to sin against God. Eli, Samuel's coach, did nothing to stop them.

One night God spoke directly to Samuel, and from that time on God guided Samuel to help lead his people back to the Lord. Coached by God and encouraged by Eli himself, Samuel confronted Eli, letting him know that God was going to punish him and his sons for their disobedience.

God had taken Eli's place as Samuel's coach. Samuel continued to be a lifelong student of God's ways. Many times he faced difficult challenges—appointing Israel's first king even as he confronted the nation for its lack of faith, and following God by appointing a replacement king while his predecessor was still in power. Samuel could have said no to God and taken the easy way out. But Samuel kept turning to God for guidance. He kept looking to his Coach, and God guided him every step of the way.

Questions for Reflection or Discussion

1. Who in your life is coaching you in the ways of God?
2. What does it mean for you to be set apart for God?
3. In which area of your life do you need to seek God's guidance?

READY WHEN THE COACH CALLS

MICHAEL

I loved playing on my hockey team. I knew that I wasn't one of the best players and understood why I didn't get to play a lot. I had a great time though. I learned a lot by playing against players better than I was, and really improved my skills even without the pressure of playing during the game. Even though I knew I might never get to play in a game, I was happy to contribute in any way I could during practice. I worked as hard as I could and was determined to be ready if the opportunity ever came for me to play in a game.

It is . . . wretched to have an abundance of intentions and a poverty of action.

–Søren Kierkegaard

During one of our games, as I was sitting in my usual spot on the bench, I looked out on the rink and noticed our team had only four players on the ice. I checked the penalty box and saw no one. Then I realized my coach had been yelling at me to get on the ice and take left wing. I leaped over the boards and took my place on the edge of the circle. I worked like crazy to prove I could handle that position and became more comfortable playing as the game went on. Soon after that game, my coach began putting me in on a regular basis. It was such a privilege to show my team that I had what it took, and I finally felt I was really contributing to the team during games—not just in practice.

When I look back now, I realize how much the development of my faith has been like my hockey experience. I was always ready to learn more about God, and I had a great passion for growing in my relationship with Him. My friends knew I was a Christian, but I wasn't ready to deal with the pressure of following Christ in my everyday life. I wasn't ready to share my faith with my friends. It seemed I needed more practice time in my faith; I felt more comfortable there. In hockey, even though I wasn't sure I was ready to play, my coach threw me in the game. I've learned that God does the same thing in my everyday life, if I'm listening closely to Him.

> *Every man is guilty of all the good he did not do.*
> —Voltaire

I can't continually be "practicing" or pretending with my faith without ever really getting in the game. God will put me into situations when He needs me there, and I must always be ready to jump in and give it all I've got. As I work hard and follow God more closely, He starts to use me more and more and I become ready and open for Him to call me into action.

What I Learned

- I need to be ready when God calls me to serve Him and be a witness to others. I need to get in the game!
- In my spiritual life, practice pays off. Everyday spiritual disciplines like prayer and reading my Bible prepare me for what God has in store for me.

Questions for Reflection or Discussion

1. Describe a time you felt you were spending too much time on the bench. How did you contribute to the team despite the fact that you weren't playing?

2. What is God calling you to do that you aren't sure you are ready to deal with yet?

3. Everyday spiritual disciplines can prepare you for God's plans for your life. What discipline do you need to commit to right now: reading your Bible, solitude, prayer?

Excellence IN ACTION

SAMUEL: *Faithful in the Midst of Disobedience*

1 Samuel 2:27–3:1
Out of obedience to the commitment she made to God before Samuel was born, Samuel's mother, Hannah, brought him to live and learn at the tabernacle instead of following in his father's footsteps as a farmer. Imagine what Samuel felt as he was dropped off at a strange, unfamiliar place away from family, friends, and everything he knew, at such a young age.

At the tabernacle, Samuel had a good coach but bad teammates. Eli's sons used their positions as a way to take what they wanted—even if it was against God. They took sacred food for themselves, used their authority to threaten men, and used their influence to seduce women who were serving God. They were treating the positions the Lord gave them with contempt. It was Eli's job to stop any actions against God at the tabernacle, but he failed to restrain his sons.

Samuel saw his coach have one set of rules for him and another set of rules for his sons. Eli was teaching one thing and doing—or not doing—another. Samuel had to listen to his coach even when Eli was not doing what was right.

In the midst of sin at the tabernacle community, Samuel chose to continue to minister before the Lord. Samuel chose to listen to the truth that his coach Eli was instructing him about, even though Eli himself (regarding his sons) was not following his own advice.

Questions for Reflection or Discussion

1. What did Samuel do when he was confronted with the choice to follow in sin or follow in obedience?
2. What was Eli's sin before God?
3. When you see something wrong, how should you respond?

LEADING UP

KARINA

> *Character is made in the small moments of our lives.*
> —Phillips Brooks

I had been trying to share my faith with one of my teammates, Ally, all year. Halfway through the season, I finally got the courage to explain to Ally how I had become a Christian. I decided I would bring it up during practice that day.

As we were in the dugout and I was talking with Ally about how my faith made me feel more whole, I suddenly heard a shout from the field. "Karina!" my coach hollered at me from outside the dugout. I looked up at him. His face was flushed. "When you're in the dugout, talk baseball!"

I felt a blush creep up my own neck as I replied calmly, "I was only trying to talk to Ally about my faith."

Coach only glared at me. "There's no room for any of your religious talk in the dugout!"

I was angry and hurt. I felt he had insulted me and, worse yet, insulted God. I wanted to yell back at him, to tell him that I could say whatever I wanted. "Coach, this is important to me," I started to say. I could see that my coach was only getting angrier. My heart was pounding as I said, "I don't think it's wrong to talk about God." I could hear anger and disrespect in my voice as soon as I said it. I thought of the verse in Romans 13:5: "Therefore, you must submit, not only because of wrath, but also because of your conscience." I knew my coach didn't understand why I felt God was important, but I had to respect him.

My coach didn't look happy. I knew I shouldn't have been talking during practice, and beyond that, I had been disrespectful when he called me on it. My inappropriate behavior was no way to share God with him. I cleared my throat and took a deep breath. "Coach, I'm sorry if I spoke disrespectfully. I didn't feel that it was wrong to share my faith with Ally. I can't promise that I won't talk about it again, but I won't let it interfere with our playing."

> *The essential and the helpful thing can be said in a few words.*
> —Dietrich Bonhoeffer

"Good enough, Karina," Coach said as he turned away.

I took a deep breath. The confrontation was over. God had stopped me and reminded me to be in control and respectful as I led upward to my coach. God had also given me the boldness to talk about my faith with my friends and my coach. I knew that this conversation wasn't finished, but through my actions I was able to show everyone a little bit more of how Christ was working in me, and as I walked off the field that day I could tell that even my coach was now more interested in my story, my relationship with God.

What I Learned

- At times, I will notice those in authority doing something wrong, and it will be appropriate for me to comment to these authority figures about their actions in a positive and constructive way. That's called leading up.

- By controlling my anger, I was able to humbly and respectfully lead up to my coach and help him and my teammates understand my faith.
- There will be many times in my life when I will disagree with others. However, disagreeing respectfully and honoring the other person will get me further with my point, and it's what God calls me to do.

Questions for Reflection or Discussion

1. How do you feel when you disagree with your coach?
2. How do you guard against being disrespectful?
3. What are some practical ways you can honor and respect leaders and coaches?
4. How do you balance your integrity as a Christian while still honoring coaches and leaders who aren't Christians?

Excellence IN ACTION
SAMUEL: *Staying Committed to His Coach*

1 Samuel 3:1–14

Samuel was in a tough situation. He had been taught what was right, but he had also seen Eli's sons making a mess of the tabernacle and all it stood for by blatantly sinning against the Lord. How would Samuel follow God and still trust and show respect to Eli, his coach?

One night Samuel was going to sleep and he heard a voice call out, "Samuel." He went to Eli and said, "Here I am. You called." Eli hadn't called him, so he sent Samuel back to his room. Samuel didn't recognize the voice of the Lord yet, but after the third time this happened, Eli realized that the Lord was calling the boy. He instructed Samuel to go back and wait; when the voice called again, Samuel was to say, "Speak, Your servant is listening." The next time the voice called Samuel, he responded as Eli had instructed him, and the Lord spoke to Samuel that night.

Even though Eli was not teaching his own sons to follow the Lord, God still used him to teach Samuel how to recognize Him. Eli helped Samuel connect to God because Samuel stayed committed to his coaching relationship.

Questions for Reflection or Discussion

1. How could Samuel stay committed to God and at the same time continue to respect Eli in his position as spiritual coach in his life?
2. Even though Eli was disobedient to God and not trustworthy, what did God teach Samuel through Eli?
3. What's most difficult about learning from someone you disagree with?

THE RIGHT ATTITUDE COUNTS

GRAHAM

Recently, I had an experience with a soccer coach that taught me a lot about patience. He was moody, angry, and unfair. He verbally fought with almost every coach on the opposing teams. He embarrassed not only himself but also our team. Many parents and the league director had discussions with him, but they didn't seem to help.

Worst of all, he seemed to care only about winning. He didn't seem to care whether we were playing as a team or even having fun.

He yelled at us if we weren't running fast enough, if we missed a goal, if a pass was off the mark, or if we did anything that wasn't perfect. It was draining playing for a coach who never encouraged us. Three of our players eventually quit because of his yelling.

I really struggled with this coach. With each practice, I grew more impatient and angry with him and developed a bad attitude, which affected how I was treating him and others on the team. At the time, I blamed my coach for everything—including my bad attitude. I didn't realize I was the one responsible for my attitude. I knew very well I couldn't deal with him myself, but I had forgotten that I followed a God with infinite patience. I finally remembered that God is patient with me all of the time! It was up to me to try to extend a bit of that patience and have the right attitude in that situation, even if the coach wasn't doing the right thing.

> *Be silent before the LORD and wait expectantly for Him; do not be agitated by one who prospers in his way, by the man who carries out evil plans.*
>
> –King David
> Psalm 37:7

I started having fun again as I went to practices and games. Even though my coach was still discouraging and impatient with us, God allowed me to be encouraging and patient with my teammates and even my coach. I know that the change in my attitude was noticeable and an example to others on the team. That soccer season helped me realize that no matter how frustrating a coach or teammate can be, I need to rely on God and remember I'm the only one responsible for my attitude.

What I Learned

- God taught me that having a good attitude and patience in a trying situation is important and an example others will notice.
- Coaches aren't perfect and sometimes it's OK to get frustrated with them. However, having a positive outlook really turned this situation around for me, even if my coach didn't improve.

- I can't blame others for my bad attitude. My attitude is something I can control, even when I can't control the situation.
- Remembering God's patience with me and having a Philippians 2:14 attitude help me and others around me!

Questions for Reflection or Discussion

1. Think about a time where you were frustrated with a coach or teammate. How did it make you feel?

> *Do everything without grumbling and arguing.*
>
> —Philippians 2:14

2. Read Philippians 2:14. Even if your coach brings a negative tone to practices and games, what practical things can you do to encourage others and help them have fun?

3. Read Proverbs 26:20: "Without wood, fire goes out; without a gossip, conflict dies down." Because this is true, how could you help the situation if you didn't complain about it with others? What do you think is the appropriate way to address how you feel?

Excellence IN ACTION
SAMUEL: *Leading Up*

1 Samuel 3:15–21

Samuel had just heard from the Lord that all the wickedness Eli's sons had done and all of Eli's failures to restrain them were going to come to bear on them. The Lord was going to take them out of their positions and judge their family.

After all the excitement of talking to the Lord and feeling all the nervousness and questions that accompanied the message God gave him, Samuel lay down till morning. What went through Samuel's mind that night as he couldn't sleep, lying there: *What does this mean? What should I do? Should I tell Eli? What should I tell Eli? What is in store for me in the future?*

Samuel arose the next morning early enough to open the doors of the house of the Lord. He had to have a lot on his mind; he had to be wrestling with what to do. He was probably thinking, *Eli is older than me. He raised me from childhood, and he taught me the ways of the Lord. He is my mentor and my coach. How can I tell him what God intends to do to his family?*

Samuel was afraid to see Eli that day, but Eli came to him and asked him what had happened. With Eli's encouragement, Samuel told him God's entire message of the wrong decisions Eli had made when he did nothing when his sons were sinning against the Lord. After everything was told, Eli had one last lesson for his student: Eli said, "He is the Lord. Let him do what is good in his eyes."

Eli did not attack his student for delivering this message; he didn't speak out against the Lord; he didn't get angry or belligerent. He turned back to God and submitted himself to whatever God saw fit to do. What a powerful message for Samuel, his student, to hear.

When Samuel found himself having to lead up and rebuke his coach, he chose to speak in humility and respect and saw God use him to bring Eli back to Him.

Questions for Reflection or Discussion

1. How do you respond when people confront you about your mistakes? What does your response tell people about God?
2. Think of a time you felt compelled to tell someone in authority over you that what he was doing was wrong. Did you go through with it? What was most challenging about the experience?
3. What does it mean to speak with humility and respect when you're speaking to your coach?

COACHES AREN'T PERFECT

J. D.

I had been playing baseball for ten years—it was my life. The summer before my freshman year, I devoted myself to the game. I worked to improve my skills through traveling teams, summer leagues, and camps and played eighty-eight games that summer. During a practice early in the school season, I injured my foot. I had no idea the extent of my injuries until I visited the doctor the next day. I found out I'd broken my foot in three different places and had months of rehab ahead of me.

I felt that all I had to look forward to was taking stats my entire freshman baseball season. I didn't even know if it was worth the trouble of being on the team. All my hopes and plans were shattered in an instant. But I felt guilty because I was almost glad that I had been hurt.

The truth was, I wasn't excited about the season. I was burned out, ready for some rest, and unsure about my connection with my coach even though he was a Christian. I knew I had to break the news to him. I prepared myself to tell him that I wanted to take this season off to heal and recuperate. I went straight from the doctor's office to the school to inform my coach that he was losing a player.

When my coach saw me, the first thing he said was, "J. D., you're late for the bus." He knew I'd been injured and that I had been at the doctor's, and he didn't seem to care. I explained to him that the doctor had told me my foot was broken. He didn't show me any compassion and simply said, "That's no excuse for being late to the game bus."

I suddenly knew that this was not a coach I could play for. This did not seem to be the way a Christian should respond. I was frustrated and hurt, and I angrily told him that I was never going to ride that bus again. I walked away and slammed the door behind me. I knew I was possibly ending my baseball career forever.

I saw that coach often because he was a gym teacher in the school, and I frequently thought about our interaction that day. I was still angry with him, and I didn't like to be around him. I was hurt by the way he handled the situation. I thought his behavior was wrong, that he should have cared for me and shown compassion for my broken foot.

But the more I thought about it, the more God revealed to me that I was just as wrong as my coach had been. Even though his comment that day was the last straw in my frustration with baseball, nothing could justify my bad attitude and the way I had handled the situation. I shouldn't have spoken from anger and resentment but, rather, with respect and truth. I should have been honest and told him that he hurt me and that I felt he wasn't being fair. Realizing this showed me that coaches can make mistakes just as I can. Just because he was the coach, I couldn't expect him to be perfect.

> *Integrity is the glue that holds our way of life together. We must constantly strive to keep our integrity. When wealth is lost, nothing is lost; when health is lost, something is lost; when character is lost, all is lost.*
>
> *—Billy Graham*

God soon gave me the opportunity to play volleyball for club and school teams, and that replaced baseball as my spring sport. But I will never forget the day I treated my coach disrespectfully. I learned that I can challenge my coaches on how they are treating me and my teammates, but they still deserve my respect. It can be hard to get along with coaches sometimes, but as an athlete and Christian, it's something God calls me to do.

What I Learned

- God taught me that patience can pay off in heated situations.
- I need to respect leaders and coaches, even when I disagree with them.

- When I get frustrated or angry, it's really important to take a close look at myself and speak wisely.

Questions for Reflection or Discussion

1. Have you ever gotten so angry that you said something you regretted later? How did it feel to know that you couldn't take back those words?

May God give us the grace to utter only those words of which we won't be ashamed afterwards.

–Desmond Tutu

2. We can often place our coaches and other leaders on too high a pedestal. They aren't perfect even if they're Christians. Is there a coach, leader, or parent you need to give grace to right now? How do you think you can encourage that person?

3. Are there any relationships now with coaches that you need to fix? How can you restore these relationships?

Excellence IN ACTION

SAMUEL: *A Lifelong Student of a Life-Giving Coach*

1 Samuel 12

Samuel grew in stature and favor with God and men. He went from a young farm boy, unsure of his surroundings and future, to become the spiritual leader of all Israel. Samuel had learned that the best leaders were those who learned how to follow. Even as Israel's spiritual leader, Samuel remained a lifelong student and servant of the Lord.

Samuel did what was right when faced with the decision to go the way of Eli's sons or go the Lord's way. He told the truth even though it was difficult. He did not choose by looking at outer appearances, as many would have done; for example, it was his decision to choose a young shepherd boy, David, to be king.

Samuel was raised to serve God and help others worship Him in the tabernacle. He was attentive to what God wanted for His people and was very troubled when they did not obey. When his own sons strayed from the ways of God in the same ways that Eli's sons had, Samuel not only knew what to do but he took action and appointed King Saul to rule over Israel.

The characteristic that defined Samuel was his sincere yearning for God. While Eli was indulging the sin of his sons, Samuel was ministering before the Lord. Surrounded by people who rejected God in their pursuit of wickedness, Samuel grew up in the presence of the Lord. When he finally recognized the voice of God, Samuel said, "Speak, for Your servant is listening." Samuel's sincere yearning for God helped him stay connected to his ultimate Coach, and his Coach's hand was on him all the days of his life.

Questions for Reflection or Discussion

Samuel had five characteristics that made him a lifelong student of God. He was teachable, honest, willing to confess his need for God, cared about others, and sincerely yearned for God. How are you doing in these areas? Rate yourself on a scale of 1 to 6 with 1 the lowest, not like you, and 6 the highest, very much like you.

1. Are you teachable?

     1   2   3   4   5   6

2. Are you honest with yourself and others?

     1   2   3   4   5   6

3. Are you humbly willing to confess your need for God?

     1   2   3   4   5   6

4. Do you care about others?

     1   2   3   4   5   6

5. Do you have a sincere yearning for God?

     1   2   3   4   5   6

SECTION 3

*You and
Your Influence*

BECKY CONZELMAN*– PROFESSIONAL CYCLIST

A PERSON OF INFLUENCE

I began cycling professionally in 2000, and quickly rose toward the top in my first two years of road cycling. Then I had the same experience in track cycling during the next two years. In my first year of track cycling, I was selected for the national team to compete in China for the fourth World Cup and then in Denmark for the world championships. Being one of the top cyclists in the country provides me with many opportunities in the course of my training to influence others. The opportunities range from brief encounters with fans while signing autographs to relationships with fellow competitors to investing in the lives of younger aspiring cyclists at the many camps and clinics I participate in.

I know God has placed me in this position of influence to make an impact for Him. Each time I get to interact with others in

---

* Becky Conzelman is a three-time gold and five-time silver national medalist in cycling. In 2002, she helped the U.S. team win the World Cup in China. At the 2002 world championships, she placed fourteenth. In 2003, she was named Rider of the Year at the Lehigh Valley Velodrome. Also, in 2004, she won the Rider of the Year award and three USCF elite national titles.

the world of cycling—whether teammates, competitors, aspiring cyclists, or fans—I try to see an opportunity to make a lasting impact in their lives—one that will challenge and encourage them to strive for success in athletics and, most importantly, in their relationships with God.

For a man with a deep-rooted faith in the value and meaning of life, every experience holds a new promise, every encounter carries a new insight, and every event brings a new message.

–Henri Nouwen

As I approached the Track Cycling National Championships, my expectations were high. My goal was to be one of the top two sprinters in the United States and win a national jersey, which would put me in strong contention for the Olympic team. I prepared long and hard for this big event; I was ready and confident that I had a real chance to achieve my goals.

The big day arrived, and I ended up placing fourth, second, fourth, and fifth in my respective events at the national championships. I was disappointed in my performance; my results didn't meet my expectations. I put my whole heart and soul into training and preparing for this event, and in the match sprint (my first event) I got fourth place. I held back the tears as I stepped up on the podium to receive my fourth-place medal. I watched in disappointment as my competitor put on the national jersey and accepted her winning gold medal, the one I had worked so hard for. In one sense, I felt honored to be on the podium with great athletes, but on the other hand, I had aimed to be on the top two steps of that podium and had worked all year for it.

As I stepped off the podium with my flower bouquet in hand and a medal around my neck, I looked up to see the smiling faces of three young girls I had coached and invested my life in during a summer cycling class at the track. In an instant, my emotions switched from disappointment to joy as Kate, Libby, and Monica ran to congratulate me. They were thrilled! The fourth-place medal around my neck weighed heavily on my heart, but to them, it seemed as exciting as winning the gold! I reached down for my flower bouquet and pulled out three flowers, one for each of them. Smiles graced their faces and hugs followed.

When I returned home, after spending time with them, all I could think of was their happy faces. I thought about the significance of what that moment had meant to them and, because of their reactions, what it had meant to me. Would pursuing my dreams and working hard encourage and inspire them to pursue greatness in their lives, and an even greater life with Christ? I hoped so. God showed me in that moment that in those three girls' lives I was able to make an impact beyond the track. I was able to do this not only by working hard at my sport but, more importantly, by investing in their lives and sharing with them my walk with Christ. I was thankful that in the midst of disappointment, I

> *Therefore since we also have such a large cloud of witnesses surrounding us, let us lay aside every weight and the sin that so easily ensnares us, and run with endurance the race that lies before us.*
>
> —Hebrews 12:1

was able to look past the circumstance and see the big picture of being an example and a person of influence in their lives.

As athletes, we're given a unique platform to be role models and share God's love with those who compete with us, look up to us, or watch us. Whether you're on the national team or not, there is always an opportunity to use the talents God has given you to be an influence on those around you. We all have an audience, and the key is whether we use that position to reflect God's love and ultimately lead others to a relationship with the Lord.

As you keep your eyes fixed on Jesus and seek to honor Him with all the talents He has given you, He will use you to be a Christlike influence on those around you. No matter what the worldly outcome is that particular day, I challenge you to be a person of influence, pointing others to Christ through your actions and words.

SPIRITUAL QUARTERBACK

WILL

I have been playing football since I was in eighth grade. My dad played quarterback in both high school and college, and I followed in his footsteps. As I grew to understand the game, I began to realize that being the quarterback could get me a lot of glory, attention, and influence. This was both a good and a bad thing because I was watched by many people, on and off the field. My grandfather—a well-known football coach—used to say, "If you talk the talk, you have to walk the walk." It seemed like such a simple concept when he said it, but I quickly found out it was easier said than done.

> *If you are a true Christian, then you are a minister. A non-ministering Christian is a contradiction in terms.*
>
> —Elton Trueblood

As my faith in Jesus Christ grew, I wanted to follow my grandfather's advice. I decided to use my platform as a quarterback for ministry purposes. Throughout high school and now in college, I've had the opportunity to start Bible studies with some of the guys from the football team. It was awesome to see all these non-Christian guys get together and discuss issues they would otherwise never talk about.

Not all the guys who joined our group were interested in God, but my relationship with them as their leader and their friend allowed them to trust me and to check it out. We met for about an hour once a week, and it was cool to see those I thought would never be interested actually come and get exposed to the Word of God for the first time.

Toward the end of one season, I injured myself and found out I wouldn't be able to play football for the rest of the year. But I needed to stay involved with these guys; my influence on the team didn't depend on whether I could play if my desire to share Jesus with others was still there. The guys on the team knew where I stood, and they all knew I was sincere and passionate about my faith. It was great to see my teammates come to understand Jesus more and be open to how He could affect their lives. God really honored my efforts—I have led a Bible study with all the football guys again this year.

As a quarterback, I'm the one who guides the team on the field. This has been a great experience for me in my football career. But a far greater experience has been my position as quarterback for my teammates in their spiritual lives—leading them to a personal relationship with Jesus Christ. Because they trusted me and could see how Christ had changed me, a few of the guys even accepted Christ into their own hearts. It was an awesome privilege to allow God to use my influence in this way.

> *You exist . . . to help them to love God better and so to serve Him by serving their fellow human beings.*
> —Desmond Tutu

What I Learned

- It can be really hard to talk the talk and walk the walk, and apart from Christ it's an impossible task. God taught me I can't do any of this under my own power, but only through Christ who strengthens me.
- God puts us into positions of influence so we can honor Him, not ourselves. As leaders on our teams, we represent Christ both on and off the field. I need to constantly strive try to live a life like Christ's so that people might see Him through me.

Questions for Reflection or Discussion

1. Read 2 Corinthians 2:14–17. How does this verse relate to your own life? To your influence?
2. Our relationship with God should be noticeable to others. How do your teammates and friends see Christ in you?
3. Will was able to use his position on his team to influence others. How are you using your influence? What are some steps you can take to use it more effectively?

Excellence IN ACTION
ESTHER: *An Unexpected Influence*

**Esther
2:1–9**

Esther was a Jewish orphan being cared for by her cousin Mordecai. She "had a beautiful figure and was extremely good-looking" (v. 7). King Xerxes, the king of 127 provinces at that time, was seeking a new queen. Esther was chosen as one of the women brought to the palace for the king to choose from. As soon as she arrived at the palace, she was considered the favorite and was given the best of everything. Over time she won the king's heart and became the queen.

Esther had risen in influence. She didn't let that get to her, however. She remembered her family and her people, the Jews. More importantly, even though she was a queen, she remembered that she was still a servant of God.

Esther always had influence in the world she lived in; now her influence increased dramatically. God made her a queen, and with the increase of influence came an increase in her responsibility to honor God in all she did. Esther was given an opportunity to show what she was made of: While others around her were clamoring for more influence with the king, Esther stayed connected to God, still aware that she was really a servant and that a servant needed to obey. During her reign as queen, she had the choice to play it safe and save herself or risk everything and save her people. When most people would have taken the easy way out, she decided to honor God and use her influence for His glory, even putting herself at the risk of death.

Esther was given increased influence so she might use it, and use it she did!

Questions for Reflection or Discussion

1. We all have influence on some level, whether with one person or one thousand. In which areas of your life do you have opportunities to influence others? How do you see God using you in those areas?

2. With influence comes responsibility to stay connected to God so He might direct you. It was important in Esther's life to keep her influence and power in proper perspective. Why is that perspective important?

3. What, or who, in your life helps you keep a proper perspective about your influence?

OTHERS ARE WATCHING

JESSICA

I was born with problems that affected the motor skills on the left side of my body. At one point, I had surgery to lengthen one of my Achilles tendons, a part of the body commonly affected by my disorder. At an early age, my parents got me involved in competitive running to strengthen my legs and prevent me from having to undergo another surgery. I ran track in grade school and junior high and added cross-country in high school. Running became more than physical therapy for me; it became something I truly enjoyed, something that was a part of me and helped define who I was.

While running had become a huge part of my life, I was never very good at it. I was the standard back-of-the pack athlete. I did have a very competitive nature, and even though I enjoyed running most of the time, at times I became very frustrated that my athletic ability didn't seem to match up with my high (and sometimes unrealistic) expectations for myself. I struggled with the inconsistencies I saw in my life and sometimes wondered why I continued to compete. I had to work hard not to let the frustration deter me from participating in the sport I loved.

> Our attitude and prayer is that everything we say and do may bring glory to Jesus Christ who loves us and gave himself for us.
>
> —Paul Little

Often, I went to my friends for support when I got frustrated. I had a series of conversations with one classmate. A standout in football, basketball, and baseball, he always played to win. He could never figure out why I continued to run because it was quite obvious to both of us I would never win a race I entered. "Jessica, you should only run races you can win," he told me. "If you can't win and you know you won't win, why do you run at all?" That bothered me, especially since I didn't have an answer that satisfied either of us. I just wasn't willing to give up my running, and that's all I knew.

By my senior year, I had been competing for many years and was potentially facing the end of my athletic career. I still wasn't sure why I continued to run when I never won but had long since given up on trying to understand why I felt called to run. I loved to compete and gave it everything I had each time I raced, and I wanted to honor God through my efforts.

God honors our efforts when our purpose is authentic, but sometimes we don't see the effect of our work right away. After all the years of not knowing why I chose to continue to compete rather than run recreationally, the answer came suddenly.

Several of my teammates and classmates came to me during my last semester to tell me what an inspiration I had been to them and how they could see Christ's work in me. One comment from a teammate hit me in a special way: "I've seen you work twice as hard to achieve the same results as other people, and it has challenged me to work harder. You showed me that I can do the things I set out to do if I really have my heart in it. God has definitely used you to help others do their best, and I want to thank you for being an example to the rest of us." Now, people had made comments before about my running, but that was truly the first time I realized to what extent God had chosen to use me to challenge others to excel and work hard in every part of life.

I will probably never win a race, but God has used my efforts to honor Him to spur others on to win their own races, both on and off the track.

> *Those who trust in the Lord will renew their strength; they will soar on wings like eagles; they will run and not grow weary; they will walk and not faint.*
>
> *—Isaiah 40:31*

What I Learned

- One of the biggest parts of being on a team is lifting one another up and each teammate using his or her abilities to strengthen one another.
- God honors how hard I try rather than how good I am compared to other people.

Questions for Reflection or Discussion

1. God has given you gifts and abilities to make a difference on your team. Sometimes, though, it can be hard to see your impact right away. What are some of the gifts you bring to your team? How might your gifts help your team in the long run?

2. Jessica wanted to honor God through her running. Because of that, her efforts paid off. How do your athletic efforts and abilities honor God and influence your teammates?

3. Do you agree that how hard we try is more important than how well we do compared to others? Why or why not? How do you keep this in mind when others do better than you?

Excellence IN ACTION
ESTHER: *Chosen to Influence*

**Esther
2:10–18**

Esther surely could have felt that she had been forgotten. She was a young girl from a people who were a minority in the land where they lived. She had no real immediate family. She lost her mother and father and was being raised by her cousin. Now she had even been taken from the only family she had left and was put in line to see if this foreign king she didn't know would pick her for his wife.

Esther probably had mixed emotions as she entered the king's palace—glad she was finally picked for something, saddened she was taken from the only family she knew, nervous about the future. She was sure of two things though: where she came from and the God she belonged to.

Her preparations to meet the king were long and extensive. With each passing day she worried that all the preparation and hard work might not be enough to catch the favor of the king and be chosen as queen.

When it was her turn to meet the king, Esther won the favor of everyone she came in contact with. She had to be scared, nervous, anxious, and excited all at the same time. Even though it was probably challenging, she also had to be confident that God would take care of her and that He had put her there for a reason. The king was attracted to Esther more than any of the others, so he chose her to be queen of his entire kingdom.

The young, seemingly forgotten orphan girl, who probably had some influence in her own world, had now been elevated to a position that influenced the whole kingdom. Esther trusted God and was given influence and responsibility far greater than she had had before.

Questions for Reflection or Discussion

1. How do you think Esther felt to be chosen queen of the entire kingdom?
2. How does it feel to know that God has chosen you to have influence where He has placed you? What specifically do you think this means for you?
3. Just as Esther took time and hard work to prepare herself before she met the king, what can you do to prepare spiritually for when God may ask you to use your influence?

FORGETTING GOD

ANDREW

During my freshmen year I was playing middle linebacker and fullback for my school. During the summer practices, I was moved up to the varsity roster. I was nervous, but I knew this was where God wanted me and I wanted to honor Him through this opportunity.

The summer practices went great, and I was performing really well. I quickly lost focus on God—even though it was God who had given me abilities and opportunities. I took all the credit for myself. I started bragging to my family and friends, and I used my position on the team to make myself look better, not to influence others. I pretty much forgot about my relationship with God.

Toward the end of the summer, I had muscle pains in my back. It was nerve–racking, and I could feel God tugging on me to change my attitude and to start focusing on Him again. But our season quickly started and I was playing well. I continued to be far from humble about my skills on the field. I had completely lost all my focus on God. During a really important game, I was blocking for our running back on a sweep play when a defensive end rolled into my knee. I had blown out the ACL and MCL in my knee. I tried to play, but my coaches and trainer wouldn't let me.

> *I may be the best in the world, but I am only jumping into a sandpit.*
>
> —Jonathan Edwards (triple jumper)

The next weeks brought appointment after appointment with doctors. After an MRI, my orthopedic surgeon told me I couldn't play for at least six months and had to undergo reconstructive surgery. The doctors decided to use part of my hamstring to repair my ACL. Soon after the surgery, I began physical therapy to regain the muscles in my leg.

It was a really hard time. I felt God had broken me down to teach me some things. I had the chance to use my position on the team to influence and encourage others, but instead I had gotten only a big head! I had forgotten to be the servant God had called me to be and had not used the abilities He had given me.

During months of therapy and a full year of sitting through second string and starting from scratch, I began to realize my responsibility: to honor God through my playing and give Him the credit for my successes. After a lot of prayer, patience, and hard work, I came back in full force my junior year and was an all-conference player! I knew God had given me this second chance, and I had learned to stay focused on Him. He taught me I should always be humble and never forget He gave me the ability to play. Everything started to work out better once I understood those lessons.

From this experience God gave me a verse I always remember:

"'Whoever exalts himself will be humbled, and whoever humbles himself will be exalted'" (Matt. 23:12). I need to be humble and honor God through the abilities He has given me. I also learned to use the influence I have on my team to glorify God, not myself. By trying to be a servant of others and care for them, I have been able to keep the right focus and to succeed in my athletics. But, more importantly, I have experienced success in my relationship with God and my efforts to influence others in my school.

> *God sends nobody away empty, except those that are full of themselves.*
>
> –D. L. Moody

What I Learned

- Being successful in sports doesn't give me the excuse to be proud. God gave me abilities, and I should try to honor Him with them.
- Staying focused on God helps me to remember to serve others and stay humble.

Questions for Reflection or Discussion

1. Matthew 23:12 reads, "'Whoever exalts himself will be humbled, and whoever humbles himself will be exalted.'" What does this verse tell you? Write this verse on a note card and place it somewhere to remind you of the proper attitude to have this week.

2. What abilities has God given you? When you compete, do you feel you honor God through your talent? Is it easy for you to give God credit for your skills? How do you give God credit?

3. How are you currently using your athletic skills to glorify God? Are you able to serve and invest in others in the midst of your playing? Whom are you trying to influence for Jesus, to encourage a closer relationship with Him? What steps do you need to take to do that?

Excellence IN ACTION
ESTHER: *Time to Choose*

| Esther 3–4 |

King Xerxes had chosen Esther to be queen of his entire kingdom, and with this choice her influence continued to grow. Still, in the kingdom others clamored for increased influence and power. One of those seeking influence was Haman.

Haman, a member of the king's nobles, was finally appointed to one of the top positions in the king's court. He let the position go to his head. He wanted the other nobles and people of the kingdom to bow down to him as he passed, to pay him homage. He thought his position and influence with the king made him better than everyone else.

Mordecai, Esther's cousin, was sitting in his usual place at the palace gate, awaiting news of how Esther was doing, when Haman came by. All the people bowed to Haman except Mordecai. This enraged Haman; he wanted to kill not only Mordecai but all his people, the Jews. Haman persuaded the king to sign a decree that would mean death to all Jews.

Haman had no idea that Esther was a Jew, and neither did the king. Mordecai did, though, and as he heard the terrible news, he immediately sent word to Esther. He was in danger, and not only he but the whole Jewish people. He asked Esther to intercede with the king to save her people.

Queen Esther heard the news and had a choice. She knew the punishment for going to the king uninvited could be death, but if she waited for the king to call for her, it could mean death for her people and her cousin Mordecai. Esther's decision—go to the king and save Mordecai and her people, or stay silent and keep her life, her influence, and her power.

Queen Esther, with the encouragement of her cousin Mordecai and after three days of fasting and prayer, decided to use the influence God gave her. She would go uninvited into the king's presence even though it could cost her life.

Many of us underestimate what we personally can do to influence others. Esther did, and if she hadn't made the right choice to use her influence, it would have led to a terrible tragedy.

Questions for Reflection or Discussion

1. At this stage of your life, how is God calling you specifically to use your influence with others?

2. Esther had hard choices to make and fears to overcome to use her influence. What are some of your difficulties and fears as you decide how and when to use your influence on your team and at school?

3. Queen Esther had Mordecai to help her stay focused, to encourage her, and to remind her of what she could do. Who in your life does that for you?

SETTING AN EXAMPLE
CAMILLE

During my senior year, I was the captain of our dance team. Girls on the team took turns coming up with the routines we would perform at competitions. On our team, before each competition the dancers had to audition for the new routine.

Before one competition, when I auditioned, the girls judging the tryouts told me I didn't know the routine well enough and therefore wasn't allowed to perform on Friday's team. But I did know the routine, and I had performed it perfectly. A few days before that, one of the girls and I had argued during a practice. I thought that by keeping me out of Friday's competition, she was trying to get me back.

I could tell the other girls on the team sensed something was up. Even my coaches were confused and didn't understand what was going on. They pulled me aside and told me I had done the routine perfectly and they were going to talk to the judges. They didn't know about our fight. I told them I accepted the results and they shouldn't worry about it.

Bless those who persecute you; bless and do not curse.

—Romans 12:14

That night I prayed that God would give me the wisdom to handle the situation appropriately. I knew younger team members were watching me and would notice how I responded to what had happened. The next day, I went to the girl I had fought with and asked if we could talk. I apologized for having argued with her. I told her I would accept the results and wouldn't do the routine, but I wanted to know that her decision wasn't because of the fight but because she really felt I wasn't prepared. She told me it wasn't anything to do with us; she thought I wasn't good enough for the competition.

That was hard to take, and I still felt her decision was personal and not based on my performance. I had never been out of a competition, but as a leader on the team and as an example to my teammates, I believed I should step back and accept it. My coaches were surprised and angered by the situation, yet sitting out at the competition, handling it right, and not making a big deal about it allowed me to show I was different.

God helped me handle this situation and be an example to my team and coaches. I had opportunities to talk to many of my teammates about struggles they were having, and my experience allowed me to relate to my teammates who weren't selected for later competitions.

What I Learned

- My teammates see how I respond in unfair situations. My behavior can set an example for them, and I want it to be a good one.
- It was important for me to confront my teammate individually and not make a big deal about it in front of others. Even though things didn't go according to my plans, I know I did the right thing.
- We can't control everything that happens to us, but we can ask God to give us the right response—and attitude.

> *Darkness cannot drive out darkness, only light can do that. Hate cannot drive out hate, only love can do that.*
> —Martin Luther King Jr.

Questions for Reflection or Discussion

1. Has a coach or teammate ever treated you unfairly? How did you respond? Would you have been able to respond the same way Camille did?
2. Can you think of times when Jesus was treated unfairly? Read Luke 23:33–35. How did Jesus respond to the cruelty of other people?
3. Think about the people on your team who may look up to you. How can you set an example for them this week?

Excellence IN ACTION
ESTHER: *Courage to Follow Through*

Esther 5–8

Haman, a self-seeking noble of high rank in the king's court, had duped the king into signing a decree that would bring death to the queen's cousin Mordecai and all the Jewish people. Queen Esther, with all her influence, had to do something.

Esther decided to go uninvited into the king's court to beg for her people's survival. Everyone knew that going into the king's court uninvited was against the law and punishable by death. She had decided she would risk all. Her courageous attitude is found in Esther 4:16: "'If I perish, I perish.'"

Those words were strong and powerful, coming from a young orphan girl, but they were only words. Now that she knew what she had to do, she still needed the courage to follow through on her words.

After she fasted and prayed for three days, she put on her royal robes, prepared herself, and entered the king's inner court. She knew it might be her last time walking those halls, the final moments of her power and influence, and the last day of her life. It would have been easy to turn around and go back to the safety, power, and influence she had as queen in the palace.

The king was shocked and surprised by Esther's appearance in his court. But instead of a death sentence, Esther found favor with the king, as he forgave her for coming uninvited. He asked Esther what was so important that she would risk her life to request it. After one failed attempt, she finally told the king everything. He was furious that Haman would do such a thing. The king figured out a way to save his queen, Mordecai, and the Jewish people, but Haman didn't fare as well.

Queen Esther showed great courage in her attempt to save her family and obey God. She used her influence for the good of others and to honor God.

Questions for Reflection or Discussion

1. How do you think Esther felt as she prepared to go to the king? Was there ever a time you felt like Esther as you were preparing to use your influence? What was it like for you?

2. Sometimes doing the right thing means you have to risk it all,

as Esther did. What are some areas that you have dealt with or are dealing with now that require a courageous faith to follow through?

3. Esther spent time with God before she went to see the king. How do you prepare when you're facing adversity? What can you learn from Esther's example?

INVESTING YOUNGER
STEVEN

I grew up playing basketball and I enjoyed it. God gave me abilities that made me one of the best on my team. I was entering my senior year and knew I had the opportunity to influence my team for Christ. I invested a lot of time and energy in basketball and my teammates. We spent many hours together playing ball and just doing life together. They knew where I stood in my relationship with Christ, and many of them were open to hearing about it. I even helped to start a pregame share time with the varsity team, before each game, which most of the team attended.

Halfway through the season, one of the coaches who was a Christian asked me to give a pregame message to the freshman basketball team. I thought it would be another opportunity to share my story with others who hadn't heard it yet. In order to give this message, I had to be at school really early on Saturday morning! The night before, the varsity squad had a conference game against a team that was battling us for the championship. There was a lot riding on this game, and there was a ton of pressure on me to perform well. Unfortunately, my teammates and I all played poorly that night and we lost. All I wanted to do was go to my room and get away from everything and everyone.

My mom came to my room to see how I was doing and to remind me about the commitment I made to the freshman coach for the next morning. I told her I wasn't going and wanted her to call and tell him. Fortunately she refused and I had to go. As I showed up early the next morning, it was the last place I wanted to be. After praying to God for strength and a different attitude, I shared with the guys my spiritual story and my feelings about the game last night. I was amazed at the reaction. They were attentive the whole time I spoke and were hanging on every word I said. After I finished, a few of the guys told me they were interested in spending more time with me and learning about God.

You are the salt of the earth. . . . You are the light of the world.

—Jesus Matthew 5:13–14

As I walked away from the school that morning, God showed me a whole new group of guys I could reach out to. The freshman basketball players looked up to me as an older player and were interested in what made me different. I was glad I had kept my commitment and had spoken with them that morning; I was pumped to see the excitement from these young guys. God used a disappointing performance to show me He can use me even at my lowest point if I'm obedient and faithful. We can grow as leaders by learning to deal with failure and by seeing that God is there with us. He can use us because others are watching even more closely after a big loss to see how we react in that circumstance.

They will almost always treat you as if you were royalty. . . . But please remember that you are there to serve them.

—Desmond Tutu

The rest of that year, I tried to make it a point to invest in some of those younger guys on the team. They were eager and willing to work on whatever I encouraged them to do. They were open to going to church and learning about God and how they could have a relationship with Him. God taught me that I can use my influence and position in sports beyond what I can see to make an impact on younger guys who might look up to me for my athletic abilities. All I needed to do was make an effort to enter into their world and invest some time sharing my life with them.

What I Learned

- God can grow me into a better person through failure and disappointment.
- There are people in my circle of influence I may not be noticing. I hadn't thought before about reaching out to younger players, and it really paid off.
- It's important to keep commitments you make. You never know how God might use them!

Questions for Reflection or Discussion

1. When you're disappointed or frustrated after a losing game, does your behavior still reflect God? What can you do to make sure you represent Christ in your playing? What does that look like?
2. Matthew 5:16 says, "'In the same way, let your light shine before men, so that they may see your good works and give glory to your Father in heaven.'" What does this verse say to you? How do your teammates see God shining through you?
3. Are there younger people you could invest in? How could you reach them this year? What are the first steps you need to take?

SECTION 4

You and Your Relationships

NANCY SWIDER-PELTZ SR.*

NANCY SWIDER-PELTZ JR.*

TRAINING PARTNERS

NANCY SWIDER-PELTZ SR.

Proverbs 27:17—"Iron sharpens iron, and one man sharpens another"—has become a theme verse for my daughter and me. Even though I have competed in four Olympic Games in speed skating, I believe my biggest achievement in sports came as I stepped on the ice to compete at my eighth Olympic trials alongside my daughter.

Nancy Swider-Peltz Sr. was a four-time U.S. Olympian in speed skating on the 1976, 1980, 1984, and 1988 teams. She has been on eight world championship teams, broken two world records, and coached four Olympians. Nancy has also reached elite levels in cycling, swimming, and triathlon.

Nancy Swider-Peltz Jr. competed in the U.S. Olympic speed-skating trials in 2001, only eighteen months after she started skating. Skating for the U.S. Junior National Team, she was the fastest in the world for a four-race combined total in her age group. In 2004, she made the Senior U.S. World Cup Team in the 3,000 meters.

Nancy Jr. was never interested in skating (her sport was actually swimming) until she received a pair of skates as a gift and decided to try them a few times. When she asked to go to a speed-skating camp with two girls I was coaching, I was surprised and said, "No way!" For Nancy's whole life I had made a conscious effort to not push her toward skating. I was not going to let anyone say, "You forced your kid into skating." If this was something she was going to do, it had to come from her. Then I realized that moment had come. Nancy was making her own decision to become a speed-skating competitor. Eighteen months later, both of us would be competing together and against each other in the Olympic trials.

> Deliberate efforts to help one another grow in the Christian practices require commitment and constancy.
>
> —Dorothy Bass & Craig Dykstra

The time leading up to the trials included a lot of hard training, which fortunately I was able to do with my daughter and one of my students, Maggie. One of the most significant things I've learned over my many years as an athlete and coach is that it's vital to train with other athletes. We spurred each other on, kept each other motivated, and held the standards high for each other. Speed skating is often seen as an individual, cutthroat sport. But to be the best, skaters need training partners.

I believe very strongly in the importance of training in groups of three. Ecclesiastes 4:12 says, "A cord of three strands is not easily broken." If two people are training together and one is sick or not motivated, it's hard for one teammate to motivate the other. If three are training together, the two who are doing well can work together to boost the third person. The quality of training improves in groups of three.

Being a part of this training team of three helped keep me going. I had an important role to play. I was experienced in how to think, train, and handle the pressure. I could motivate Nancy and

Maggie by modeling the discipline and effort it takes to make it to the Olympics—how to think through situations, train, and make decisions. In the same way, they pushed me to give my best, not just a mediocre performance. It's not a coincidence that skaters who have become the best have all trained with others. The team of three who train together is not easily broken!

For the five weeks leading up to the trials, and at the trials, Nancy Jr. and I were both very nervous. We had put a lot of time, effort, and training into this event. It is nerve-racking because one injury, one cold, one bad day could take us out of the running. All of our work to that point could have achieved nothing.

We finally made it to the day of the trials, held at the Olympic Oval in Kearns, Utah. Here I was, forty-five years old, competing in my eighth consecutive U.S. Olympic speed-skating trials alongside my fourteen-year-old daughter—the first time in history that a mother and daughter had competed together in the Olympic trials.

When the skaters were randomly paired by computer for the first race, we were paired to skate together! It was amazing to look up at the board and see Nancy Swider-Peltz Jr. and Nancy Swider-Peltz Sr. right next to each other. Lining up at the start against my training partner, my daughter, was an intense moment filled with a flood of emotions. In that race I beat Nancy Jr., but that was the last time I ever did!

Being at the Olympic trials together was a great experience for us. We will talk about it for the rest of our lives.

NANCY SWIDER-PELTZ JR.

People often ask me how I feel about having my mom as my coach. They wonder if it puts a strain on our relationship. I would say just the opposite; it's amazing how well it works. The main reason is that my relationship with my mom as both my coach and one of my training partners is based on our relationship with Christ. This is our common ground, the foundation that helps us inspire each other.

It's really amazing how God put my mom, Maggie, and me together. It was perfectly orchestrated. The level of intensity couldn't have been there if the three of us weren't pushing each other to our limits. There's no way I could have endured the hard workouts alone.

My favorite verse of Scripture is Proverbs 27:17: "Iron sharpens iron, and one man sharpens another." I have experienced this kind of relationship with my mom, not just in athletics but in many aspects of my life. We spend a significant amount of time together traveling in the car for training. Through our time and training together, I've been sharpened in my life and in my faith.

> *A cord of three strands is not easily broken.*
> —Ecclesiastes 4:12

In my faith journey, the need to "train" with partners is even more essential. It's important to train in my spiritual life as well as in athletics. If I want to improve in a sport or skill, I have to train hard and give my all, even when I don't feel like it. This is the same in my spiritual journey. I need to surround myself with people who will take me in the right direction. We tend to become like those we spend the most time with, and Hebrews 10:24 encourages us: "Let us be concerned about one another in order to promote love and good works." My mother and I challenge you to find a small group of teammates, friends, or family to be your training partners in the spiritual arena. You need the sharpening relationships Proverbs 27:17 talks about. When you're weak or struggling, your training partners can pick you up and help you along. When you're doing well, you in turn can lift your partners and help them persevere. Strong, sharpening relationships are essential for you to become a fully devoted follower of Christ.

KEEPING A PROMISE
DANA

O ne day at school, I heard there would be tryouts for the girls' volleyball team. I really wanted to make the team, but my experience was limited, and I knew it would be difficult. I tried to use God to get what I wanted. *Dear God,* I prayed, *if you let me make the team, I'll do it all for You. I will tell the whole team about You, God!* That was probably the most selfish prayer I had ever uttered because I knew that my real intention was not to glorify God but to glorify my social status.

Almost to my surprise, I made the team! Suddenly, I had quite a promise to keep. Practices started the next week. The girls were great, and I loved the chance to become their friends. After a few games, we were all really close. We'd have team sleepovers and talk for hours.

After a few weeks, I realized I had never mentioned my faith, so I began to look for opportunities to talk about it. At one of our gatherings, I came on pretty strong about my belief in God. My teammates were taken aback and then responded with some really tough questions, asking why a good God would allow pain and war. All I knew was that I really wanted to share God with them, but I didn't know how to answer their questions. They reacted so forcefully that I decided I would never so conspicuously bring up my beliefs to the team again.

> *Go into all the world and preach the gospel, and if necessary, use words.*
> —St. Francis of Assisi

Instead, I decided to simply live what I believed. I tried to be a servant to the team—taking cupcakes to practice, running to get the stray ball, making sure I talked to everyone, even the girl no one talked to. My teammates began to notice. Through this, I was able to quietly show Christ to my team and a few girls in particular.

Sarah and Mary were not Christians. We became great friends on the team and were teammates the next year. The three of us were very close and did everything together.

God, who provides us with every good thing, leads us to the truth, by gradually accustoming our darkened eyes to its great light.

—Basil the Great

When the season ended, there were no longer team sleepovers, but now there were "Dana, Mary, and Sarah sleepovers." I had many opportunities to share the gospel with them, but I didn't want to scare them off. I continued to witness to them through my actions and our friendship; I was there for them as a friend.

Before the school year even began, a girl from our school was struck by a car and died a few days later. I knew Megan through my youth group, and her death made me realize something. Mary and Sarah's lives were fragile, too, and they needed to know about Christ. The season continued, and I tried to be very open about my faith even though it wasn't comfortable for me. Because of our friendship, I was able to tell my story and challenge my teammates in their beliefs. Sarah and Mary respected my faith; they didn't agree, but they respected me because they knew I cared for them. They had noticed I acted differently from others, and now they knew why.

That year, Sarah came to a youth group camp with me and decided to ask Jesus into her life. Last year, as a high school junior, Mary made the same decision. God did have a plan for me on the volleyball team, but I had to learn how to best share God with my friends. I learned to be patient and reach out the way God had uniquely designed me to—through an authentic friendship with Mary and Sarah.

What I Learned

- I had tried to use God for my own purposes. God showed me there was more to my relationship with Him than that. I saw how God could use me to make a difference for Him.

- I had a huge desire to share God with my friends, but I had to learn the right way to approach them. God showed me that evangelism worked best in relationships. By serving them and being their friend, I found opportunities to show Christ to them.
- God uniquely designs us for evangelism. We all have different ways to share with our friends. It was exciting for me to find a way that was comfortable and effective.
- Often, we look at non-Christian friends as projects—people to help. It can be easy to forget the importance of friendships.

Questions for Reflection or Discussion

1. How has God designed you to best share your faith?
2. How do you connect and relate with non-Christians? Do you care about them regardless of their choices on faith?
3. How could you serve your teammates this week? Who do you need to be intentional about reaching out to and sharing your faith with?

Excellence IN ACTION
PETER: *Rock or Reed?*

1 Peter 5:8–11

Peter, the fisherman, had a wide-ranging relationship with Jesus. In his first encounter with Jesus on his boat, Peter first questioned Jesus' command, then followed it and finally fell down at Jesus' feet out of respect. Jesus at that time told Peter that he would, from then on, fish for men. Peter's relationship with Jesus was sometimes as strong as a rock and other times swayed like a reed blown by the wind.

One night when the disciples were on the lake in their boat, Peter saw Jesus coming to him on the water. After determining it was Jesus and not a ghost, he stepped out of the boat and walked to Jesus on the water.

Another time, Jesus was washing the disciples' feet, but Peter refused to let the Lord wash his feet. After the Lord explained that Peter's feet needed to be washed, Peter said, "Then not just my feet but my whole body."

At the Last Supper, when Jesus prepared the disciples for His arrest and crucifixion, Peter, who was confused and troubled, boldly stated he was ready to give his life for Jesus. Only a few hours later, he denied he even knew Jesus.

Fortunately, Peter was later reinstated by Jesus as a leader among His disciples. Peter—the one who had spoken so boldly to Christ and the one who had boldly denied Christ three times—was now committed more firmly than ever to boldly proclaim Christ's message to all who would listen.

Peter yearned for God, and he pursued a relationship with Jesus the best way he knew how. Jesus' and Peter's relationship saw much joy and pain. Peter, the rock that Jesus could count on, at times was a reed blowing in the wind. But one thing was certain: Jesus called Peter His friend.

Questions for Reflection or Discussion

1. What kind of relationships are you looking for from those you're close to?
2. Most of the time in your relationship with Christ, do you feel more like a rock or a reed?
3. What are some difficult areas for you as you try to stay in a close, rocklike relationship with Christ and others?
4. What keeps you close to God or brings you back to God when you feel you might have failed Him?

WORKING TOGETHER
KAYLIE

In my freshman year of high school, I decided to join the soccer team. I had already been playing soccer for four years. The day of tryouts came when the freshman, junior varsity (JV), and varsity teams would be selected. I walked into the gym ready to prove myself worthy of JV or hopefully even varsity. The coaches called out all the names of the girls who had paid and turned in their sheets with signatures. I was always behind on that kind of stuff, and I had to leave tryouts because I didn't have all the right forms filled out. I couldn't get to the athletic office for the next two days to get everything turned in. By that time, tryouts were over. I was placed on the freshman team because the coaches had never seen me play.

> A leader's attitude is caught by his followers more quickly than his or her actions.
>
> —John Maxwell

The first day of practice I showed up with a bad attitude because I thought I was good enough to be on JV. I was so frustrated—half of the girls on the team had never played before. I would pass them the ball and they couldn't stop it—it would roll right by. They would shoot, and the ball would either fly over the goal or go fifteen feet to the side. It was hard to play with girls who didn't have experience, and I had a terrible attitude about it. I wasn't supportive or encouraging, only frustrated!

After weeks of frustration, I decided to ask God for help. I sensed that my attitude was hurting our team unity. My attitude made me just as much a problem for our team as the girls who could barely play! I prayed for patience and kindness, that I wouldn't get angry but that I would help my teammates. I promised God I would give them a chance and believe in them. I began to work on my attitude, and after a few weeks we were actually winning games—all because of teamwork! I quickly learned that with hard work and belief in one another, great things can happen.

After changing my attitude, I was able to build relationships with the other girls. We started to have fun together, and I became friends with many of my teammates. I helped them with drills; we all learned together and began to play the game together. I hadn't realized how much my attitude affected the team because the other girls looked up to me for leadership.

And we exhort you, brothers: warn those who are lazy, comfort the discouraged, help the weak, be patient with everyone.
—1 Thessalonians 5:14

As the season went on, four of us moved up to varsity. Two of them were girls I didn't believe in at the beginning—girls I didn't give a chance at first were now my friends. God showed me I was really wrong about them and taught me that serving and working together with my teammates made all the difference.

What I Learned

• Getting frustrated and angry with my teammates doesn't help them or make me feel any better!

• By serving and encouraging others, I was able to help the team improve.

• A bad attitude can really hinder a team's success. I had to work hard and pray that God would give me patience and self-control. It was worth it in the end.

Questions for Reflection or Discussion

1. In which areas of your life do you have a poor attitude? Spend a few moments asking God for His help in this area.
2. How is your attitude at practice and at games affecting your teammates?
3. What opportunities do you have to lead and encourage others? What are some practical ways you can do this?

Excellence IN ACTION
PETER: *Stepping Out*

Matthew 14:22–33	One night after Jesus had a very long day, He asked the disciples to take the boat across the lake. Jesus was going to stay on the other side to spend time in prayer and solitude with His Father.

At about three in the morning, the disciples saw someone coming toward them on the water. Many in the boat thought it was a ghost. Jesus shouted to them, "It is I—don't be afraid." Peter said, "Lord, if it's really You, then direct me to come to You on the water." Jesus agreed, and Peter, putting his trust in his friend, stepped out of the boat.

Peter was walking to Jesus on the water! But then he got scared and started to sink. Jesus reached out His hand and brought Peter back to safety in the boat.

So was Peter a failure? He got distracted, started to sink, and needed Jesus to save him.

But there were twelve in the boat that night, and . . .

Eleven stayed quiet . . . while one spoke up, asking Jesus for direction.

Eleven stayed safe . . . while one stepped out, overcoming his doubts and fears.

Eleven stayed dry . . . while one got wet.

Eleven saw a miracle . . . while one experienced it.

Eleven were amazed at what they saw . . . while one had his life changed forever.

Peter stepped out in risky obedience, trusting Jesus, and was able to experience being out on the water with his friend, Jesus. He found himself in a desperate situation and was humble enough to cry out for help. As Peter proved he trusted Jesus, Jesus proved that He could be trusted.

Questions for Reflection or Discussion

1. In which of your relationships is God directing you to step out of the boat? What is He asking you to do? What is holding you back from doing it?
2. What do you think has been the boldest thing you've ever done in your relationship with Jesus? What did you learn about yourself when you did it? What did you learn about God?
3. What causes you to want to play it safe instead of following God with risky obedience?

GOD WANTS THE BEST FOR YOU

SAMUEL

As a freshman in high school, I had made the varsity baseball team as the starting center fielder. After a productive season leading the team in hits and stolen bases, I was looking forward to a great season of summer league as well. However, my life and baseball career were shaken up when my family decided to move from our home in Georgia to Oklahoma where my dad had taken a new job.

Upon arriving in Oklahoma, I found I had missed summer league tryouts and therefore wouldn't be able to play on the JV or varsity teams. The head coach informed me I could play on the lower team for the summer and I would have to ride the bench for a year on JV before he would consider playing me at all.

When one door closes, another opens, but we so often look upon the closed door that we do not see the one that has opened for us.

—Alexander Graham Bell

This news shook my world and upset me greatly because I believed God had given me a gift to play baseball and, more importantly, the opportunity to be a light to my baseball teammates. I was frustrated and mad at God and at my parents for moving me away from a great home and a sport I loved to a city that seemed to have no place for me. It was hard for awhile as I struggled with what to do. Because of my anger and frustration, it was hard to be around my family. I had left the only place I had ever known, the place I had friends, and now I felt my relationship with my family was strained also. I felt alone.

As frustrated and alone as I was, I kept returning to my favorite verse, Jeremiah 29:11: "'For I know the plans I have for you'—[this is] the LORD's declaration—'plans for [your] welfare, not for disaster, to give you a future and a hope.'" I really took this verse to heart. I tried to understand what God was trying to do with me. I poured out to God my anger, the pain of moving, and my sadness over baseball.

"For I know the plans I have for you"–[this is] the LORD's declaration– "plans for [your] welfare, not for disaster, to give you a future and a hope."

—Jeremiah 29:11

Soon afterward, my parents and I talked and our relationship was strengthened. The frustration that was once there toward God and my parents was gone. Through much prayer and guidance from my parents, I decided it would be best to redirect my energy from baseball to music. This decision has been one of the biggest blessings of my life. God has amazed me with many wonderful opportunities to serve Him through leading worship for my church youth ministry.

So, although I stopped playing baseball, I still love to participate in other sports. Persevering through this also enabled me to see how God used this seemingly huge setback to give me a wonderful future in serving Him through music.

What I Learned

- It's OK to be frustrated with God when things don't seem to go my way. God understands my anger and disappointment, and I can grow closer to Him through these experiences.
- Sometimes what appears to be a setback actually opens opportunities for me to do something else that will give me great joy.
- God knows what He's doing with my life—even if I can't understand it at the time. He has my best interests at heart.

Questions for Reflection or Discussion

1. Have you ever not made the team you were hoping to make and experienced what Samuel did? How frustrated were you?
2. Have you ever felt someone somehow messed up a sports opportunity for you? How did you deal with that?
3. When you have relationship problems with family or friends, what do you tend to do? What do you think you should do?
4. What steps can you take this week to be open to God's plan for you? Write down Jeremiah 29:11 on a note card and look at it during the week to help you remember that God does have a plan for you.

Excellence IN ACTION
PETER: *Actions Speak Louder Than Words*

John 13:3–17

Peter was loyal to Jesus. He was troubled at the Last Supper when Jesus got up from the table at His last meal with the disciples, got down on His knees, and started to wash their feet. Peter was troubled; he thought this work was beneath Jesus. He felt that, if anything, he should be washing Jesus' feet. When his turn came, he was hesitant to let his friend and Lord do such a task. Jesus said that unless He washed Peter, Peter could have no part of Him. Peter relented, asking Him to wash not only his feet but also his head and hands.

Peter couldn't imagine life without Jesus. He was confused as the Lord spoke that night of going away to a place where he couldn't follow. Peter asked Jesus, "Why can't I go with You?" As Jesus talked about His betrayal and arrest, Peter pledged his loyalty, saying, "I will lay down my life for You."

Jesus knew what was going to happen, so He told Peter that he, bold and reliable Peter, would disown Jesus three times. Peter was shocked and taken aback; even if he had to die with Jesus, he swore, he would never disown Him.

Later that night, a crowd came to arrest Jesus. Peter was ready to fight for his friend and Lord, but Jesus allowed the crowd to take Him without resistance.

Peter was afraid, confused, and curious. He followed the crowd at a distance and stood outside the place where Jesus was held to see what was going to happen to Him. Three times as he was waiting, he was confronted by individuals asking him if he had been with Jesus, and all three times Peter said no. Just as he was speaking the words of denial the third time, Jesus turned and looked straight at Peter. As Peter locked eyes with his friend and Lord he remembered the words Jesus spoke to him before. He went outside and wept bitterly.

Questions for Reflection or Discussion

1. Which do you value more in a friend: actions or words? Why?
2. Peter had planned to live up to the words he'd spoken earlier, but in the heat of the moment, he failed his friend. Has a friend ever let you down, or have you ever let down a friend when he or she really needed your support? How did that feel? How did it affect your relationship?
3. In your relationship with Jesus, when your actions don't match your words, what do you do to get back in a strong relationship with Him?

A NEW PERSPECTIVE

MACKENZIE

During my sophomore year I went to my school's volleyball camp. I was excited for the season to begin. Our first game was against our town rival—it was going to be a great game. During camp I decided I wanted to be one of the youngest players on the varsity team. I was really motivated to be the best I could be.

School started and tryouts began. The varsity coach said she would be watching the sophomore team to pick a few girls for varsity. I knew this was my chance. I was going to work extra hard at practices and really give it my all. I wanted that varsity spot, and I wasn't going to let anything or anybody get in the way. A few weeks went by, and I thought for sure that after our first few games I would be picked.

The Truth, even though I cannot feel it right now, is that I am the chosen child of God, precious in God's eyes, called the Beloved from all eternity and held safe in an everlasting embrace.

–Henri Nouwen

During practice before our first game, my team was doing its usual warm-up routines, which included blocking. During the drill I came down from a fake block and landed badly on my foot. As the tears started to fall, I thought my chance to play on the varsity team was gone. The school trainer said the injury looked really bad and I wouldn't be able to play in the game. I watched as we played our biggest rival—and lost.

Over the next week my foot didn't get any better, and finally my mom took me to the doctor. We found out I had been walking on a broken foot that whole week! When I arrived at practice the next day with a cast on my foot, the varsity coach pulled me aside and told me I had been first on her list to move up. I couldn't understand why this was happening now—why God was letting this happen to me. I was sad, and the hardest part was that there was nothing I could do to get back more quickly; I had months of rehab ahead. The entire season seemed like a waste to me; all of my hard work went down the drain.

If I had a piece of advice to give to a young man about where to live, I think I should say, "Sacrifice everything to live where you can be near your friends."

–C. S. Lewis

As hard as it was, God taught me a lot during this time. He taught me to have patience. In Psalm 46:10 God says, "Stop [your fighting]— and know that I am God." I had to remember that verse as I sat on the bench that year, watching and wanting to play. During one of the moments when I was really wondering why God had let this happen, I sensed that He was telling me to concentrate on building friendships with the other girls. My single-minded competitiveness would normally put my relationships with teammates on the back burner. During practices and games I started to encourage the other girls. I started to plan times for some of us to hang out. It was fun getting to know my teammates off the court. I had a great time! I developed deep relationships that season on our team, and now these girls are some of my best friends.

Being injured helped me enjoy volleyball a lot more and understand the importance of developing strong relationships with others. I had to be patient through the healing process and learn that things happen in God's time. Things don't always go according to my plans; God may have different things in store for me.

God showed me a different perspective on playing. I'm still intense and want to win, but I learned the value of playing as a team, having teammates who are also close friends.

What I Learned

- Being patient allowed me to follow God more closely.
- I can make a big impact on my team beyond playing. Building relationships with others and encouraging them has really made my team stronger and playing more fun!
- Even if things don't go according to my plans, God can have great things in store for me.

Questions for Reflection or Discussion

1. Think of a time when you felt God let you down. What was that like? What helped you overcome the disappointment? What plans did God have in store for you?
2. In which area of your life do you need to be more patient? Spend time praying about that issue and ask God to give you peace and hope for what lies ahead.

3. What are your relationships with your teammates like now? What can you do and how can you initiate times that will help to strengthen those relationships? Who is one person you can start with this week?

Excellence IN ACTION
PETER: *A Second Chance*

John 21:1–19

Peter was feeling the pain of his betrayal. Since the Crucifixion, Jesus had appeared to him with the other disciples, but Peter knew there was unfinished business between them.

Peter was a fisherman by trade, and he decided one night to fish. Two other disciples went with him. When morning came, they hadn't caught anything, and a man on the shore suggested they put their nets down one more time. They did, and the nets suddenly were overflowing with fish. As soon as the disciples figured out they were talking to Jesus, Peter jumped overboard and swam to shore, while the others followed in the boat.

Peter and the others sat by the fire on the shore and ate breakfast with Jesus. Imagine what must have been going through Peter's mind as he sat and ate with Jesus. He had to be thinking of the moment their eyes met after Peter had denied Him the third time—the hurt, the pain, the barrier that stood between them. After breakfast, Peter and Jesus had a private conversation. As they walked, Jesus asked him, "Peter, do you love me?" Peter, bold but still stinging from the memory of Jesus watching him deny their friendship, replied instantly, "Yes!" Jesus asked him this two more times, and Peter, with his heart heavy, said, "Lord, You know all things; You know that I love You."

From that day on, Peter was a rock. He led the others in proclaiming the message of Christ's death and resurrection. He delivered the message to all who would hear on the day of Pentecost, when all of Jesus' followers were anointed with the Holy Spirit, and about three thousand people came to trust in Jesus that day. Peter, the reed who had blown with the wind at Jesus' darkest hour, was now the rock on which the church would be built.

Questions for Reflection or Discussion

1. Describe a time you've had a relationship that was broken and then healed and restored. What were your feelings before and after the healing? What did you learn from that experience?
2. How does the fact that Peter—sometimes daring and sometimes deeply flawed—was still used by God to be the rock that the church was built on? Does this encourage you to pursue a relationship with Him and others?
3. Is there any unfinished business in any of your relationships, either with a friend, a teammate, or with God? What's holding you back from restoring that relationship? What can you do to start the healing process this week?

NOT ALONE

DYLAN

The Ragbrai is the *Des Moines Register*'s Annual Great Bike Ride across Iowa. Every year in July, more than twenty-thousand riders dip their tires in the Missouri River and begin the 450-mile ride across the state. It takes one week and ends with a tire-dipping ceremony at the Mississippi River. This race is something my dad and I have committed to doing together each year. Because the race is so long, my dad and I train for it throughout the entire year. I play other sports through the year, and this is probably the hardest single sporting event I've ever competed in.

Like any sport, Ragbrai requires practice, even on days when I don't feel like working. Sometimes it's hard to stay committed when I know there are twelve months ahead before this one race! Training with my dad and having his encouragement really help me to stay focused, especially when I want to put off practices or quit when it gets tough.

> *Brothers become strongly knit together when one helps another.*
> —Augustine

Finally, after many months of training, race week came. As we started, the days were long and uneventful. We would break down our tent, get something to eat, ride, eat, ride some more. At night, we would relax and read and get ready to do it all over again the next day. It felt great to finally be doing what I had prepared for all year.

The last day should be the easiest because we knew we were almost done, but this one particular year it was horrible. The night before was filled with constant thunder and lightning, and I hardly got any sleep. My dad and I woke up, determined to finish the race even when many people were quitting because of bad weather. It was a nasty and grueling day; the wind and rain were so loud I had to yell for my dad to be able to hear me at all.

If I had ridden nearly four-hundred miles and had only fifty to go, it wouldn't seem to be that hard. But that day was hard on everyone, not just me. Many moments I looked to the side of the road and saw a rider sitting on the grass, head down and bicycle upside down—the signal for the support vehicles to come to the rescue. I can truly say, though, that I never seriously considered quitting. My dad was right beside me, the whole way. We had been preparing each other for this moment all year, and I knew that with God's help and my dad's encouragement, I wasn't alone. I could make it.

I learned a lot about myself during that race. I learned that with lots of practice and a solid riding partner, I can go far beyond what I imagined I could do alone. I also got to know a lot about my dad; our relationship is deeper now and continuing to grow. I look forward to future years of training and racing with my dad.

What I Learned

- With God's help, I can do anything. Six days and more than 450 miles weren't easy, but we accomplished it!
- I was made to do life with others and to rely on my good Christian friends and my family for help along the way. With their encouragement, support, and holding me to accountability, I know I can accomplish anything I set my mind to.
- While my friends and family are a needed support system, staying close to God is the foundation of that support system.

Nothing so makes friends and rivets them so firmly as affliction; nothing so fastens and joins the souls of believers.

—John Chrysostom

Questions for Reflection or Discussion

1. Read Ecclesiastes 4:9–12. What do you think about these verses? How does this relate to your athletic training? To your life?
2. When has a friend or family member helped you pull through a difficult situation? How can you support other friends or family members now?
3. Do you know of a family member or friend who needs your support? What steps do you need to take to support that person?
4. Is there an area of your life in which you need to ask someone to keep you accountable, as in the verses you read above? Who? Ask that person this week to come alongside you and help you.

SECTION 5

You and Your Church

STEVE HOLLAND*

A LIFELONG COMMITMENT

Even when I was young, I knew that being involved in a local church was extremely important. Although my mom encouraged my church attendance, until the time I graduated from college, I was the only one in my family who consistently went to church. During my career as both an athlete and a coach, my conviction about the local church's importance has grown stronger. There is no place better than the local church when it is working right! The apostle Paul summed it up best when, at the end of his life, he wrote these words regarding his passion for and pursuit of building the local church: "I have fought the good fight, I have finished the race, I have kept the faith" (2 Tim. 4:7). I want to have that same kind of intense passion for the local church all the days of my life. The church is the place I'm going to be encouraged, equipped, and empowered to be the man God wants me to be.

✽ *Steve Holland is a former Mr. Universe, International Federation of Bodybuilders world champion, and Lightweight Mr. USA. Steve also was an all-American football player in college.*

It's great to have passion about a sport, but I have to make sure it doesn't cross the line and become an obsession. I've struggled with this because athletics demand much focus and time. When I was in training, during some seasons the demands of bodybuilding could have consumed me if I had let them. Trying to balance the

Not staying away from our meetings, as some habitually do, but encouraging each other—and all the more as you see the day drawing near.

—Hebrews 10:25

workouts, diet and nutrition, and mental concentration took so much of my energy and time that everything else seemed to fade in importance. I always tried to remind myself to keep athletics in the right perspective. God needed to be my obsession, and I needed to remember that involvement in a local church was vital to my spiritual growth. I had to strike a healthy balance: being driven and passionate about achieving my athletic goals but also always making sure that my obsession and top priority were to grow in my relationship with God.

Being involved in a local church is important for two primary reasons. First, it provides me with a strong foundation. Just as I need a strong foundation of fitness to be the best competitor I can be, so in life I need a strong biblical foundation to be the best I can be as a follower of Christ. Being actively involved in a local church provides the foundation for growing in my faith. Second, I need to be in a community that will support and encourage me as I walk my spiritual journey. None of us can avoid struggles, and during those times it is vital to be surrounded by people who will uplift, encourage, and challenge me to live up to the standards God has called me to.

Over the years I've struggled to find the church that's the best fit for me. People tend to think of me as "Steve, the Bodybuilder" rather than just "Steve, a guy trying to follow God." I want my church to be a place where people know me for more than just my athletic accomplishments. My church is a place where I can authentically grow and help others grow. God taught me over the years to never give up seeking the right church, not the perfect church but the church where I fit.

I challenge you to seek an intense consistency in every area of your life, especially when it comes

> *The local church is the hope of the world.*
>
> —Bill Hybels

to your commitment to the local church. Obviously, consistency in training for athletics is important, but this same concept applies to the rest of our lives, especially the church. It's very easy to wake up Sunday morning and think, *I'm just too tired, too exhausted. I'll go to church next week.* The problem is that next week the same thought will creep into your head and "next week" ends up being "never." My devotion to a local church will be the best commitment I make.

Many athletes are involved in parachurch ministries such as Fellowship of Christian Athletes and Athletes in Action, and those can be great experiences. These ministries can be a place to encourage others and be encouraged and minister to others as well as be ministered to. Be careful, though, that you don't forget to make active involvement in the local church your primary commitment. The Bible calls believers to build the church. It's easy to think that involvement in a campus ministry means you don't need church, but the local church is where you'll be able to grow for your entire life, not just a season of it.

If you're going to be a fully devoted follower of Jesus, you need the support of other believers—support that encourages you in your faith beyond your athletic abilities and for longer than our years in school, support that requires personal active commitment to the local church. There is no better foundation for growing in your faith than the local church when the local church is working right!

SENT OUT

JUAN

Growing up, I was always committed to church. I also loved sports; I enjoyed competing in football, basketball, and baseball.

Once I got to high school, it seemed I couldn't balance everything. My commitments to church, youth ministry, and sports were increasing to the point that I couldn't keep up. I was running from one event to the other, trying to do it all but feeling I wasn't committed to anything. I had an awesome group of friends at church who I really enjoyed hanging out and growing close to God with. I also had a great group of friends in sports, my teammates during the various seasons. I had two distinct groups of friends— two worlds—and those worlds didn't fit together.

I started feeling guilty when I wasn't able to go to youth group activities as much as I had before. Sports were taking up more and more of my time. My church friends and I were starting to feel disconnected from each other. They started to wonder where I was and why I had dropped out of our community that seemed to be so tight.

I really wanted to be able to do it all—to be committed to sports and also be a part of youth ministry. Most of the guys on my team weren't Christians; maybe I was there to reach out to them. But I had always been taught that God comes first, and that seemed to tell me that youth group was more important than my relationships with teammates. I was all set to give up playing sports and commit myself to our youth group when my youth pastor asked me to go out for breakfast. I thought he was calling to challenge me to be more committed to our youth ministry. So I thought this would be a perfect time to tell him my decision to quit sports even though I loved them.

When we got together, we started talking. He told me he knew what I was struggling with and he thought it would be best for me to stay committed to sports and my teammates. I couldn't believe what he was saying! He explained that the purpose of our youth ministry was to equip students to minister to their friends. It wasn't about being in a small group of all Christians, only talking about church things. He affirmed that God had placed me on these teams for a reason. He also reminded me that I did need other Christians to encourage me and equip me, so we worked out a time when we could meet and he would teach me to do ministry on campus with my teammates. We discussed the important church activities for me to be involved with and set up weekly equipping meetings for me and a few other student leaders. It was great!

It is with the coming of Jesus that a fuller freedom becomes available.

—Robert Banks

When I walked away from that meeting, I felt as if a huge weight was taken away. My guilt was gone. I felt affirmed that God had given me athletic talent and that I could use it to make an eternal impact. At that moment, I started to see that the two worlds I thought were miles apart were actually very close. I started to involve my friends at church with my ministry on campus to my teammates, and as a youth ministry we tried to figure out ways to reach athletes at our high school. We had some sporting events at church, and my pastor did a teaching series based on sports topics. My church friends got to know my teammates, and my teammates got to see that church, God, and Christians might have something to offer them after all.

What I Learned

- My youth ministry is there to equip me, support me, and send me into my world to reach others who are far from God.
- Even when my sports and church activities seem worlds apart, they can work together.

- God calls us to influence the world with our faith. We can't do this if we stay in our churches all day! We have to go out and serve others in order to show God to them.

Questions for Reflection or Discussion

1. How does your life at church mesh with your life in school and sports?
2. How might your youth ministry help you minister to your friends or teammates?
3. With school, sports, and church, do you ever feel stretched too far? What do you need to do to better balance all these things?
4. What are some steps you can take to bring your sports world and your church world closer together?

Excellence IN ACTION
PAUL: *Intensity for the Church*

Philippians 3

Paul had a love for the things of God his whole life. He studied under some of the most well-known religious teachers of his age. Paul was radically devoted to the faith and what it stood for.

Before Paul understood who Christ was, he looked at the group of people who followed Jesus as a threat to the church he knew, and he did everything he could to stop Jesus' teachings from spreading.

Then one day he encountered Christ and was literally struck down in his tracks. He got to know Christ personally, and his life changed forever.

With the same intensity that he had opposed Christ, Paul now promoted Christ as the only way to God. He committed himself to take the message of Christ boldly to everyone who would listen. He willingly suffered many hardships and abuse for the sake of Christ. Paul's passion as he proclaimed Christ's message was consistent: he would boldly share the truth with everyone and stand up to anyone who opposed it.

Paul's life was a life of extremes. He opposed Christ's people to the extreme, then he met Christ under extreme circumstances, and he became an extreme proclaimer of Christ's message. He had such an extreme change that his name was changed—he was no longer Saul of Tarsus but Paul the champion of the church. His life as the first and foremost Christian missionary continues to have a profound impact on the church as we know it.

Questions for Reflection or Discussion

1. What appeals to you about Paul's intensity?
2. What things in your life are you pursuing intensely? Are these things important, or are they possibly distracting you from pursuing Christ?
3. What does it take for you to keep your focus on Christ?
4. Are you significantly involved in your local church? Do you have an intense commitment to your church? Why or why not?

PUTTING GOD AND CHURCH ON THE SHELF

ERIN

I've been a Christian my whole life. I was raised in a Christian family, so I didn't know what life was like without going to church or knowing about Jesus Christ. I've also been a gymnast most of my life. I started taking gymnastic classes when I was three, and I never stopped. I don't remember life before practices and meets. Both my Christianity and gymnastics have made me the person I am. But as I got older, I grew more committed to my sport, and my relationship with God and my church slowly started to fade away. I put God on a shelf, and called to Him only when I needed something. My heart and life were filled with competing and training; God and church were no longer my priorities.

> *To have a well-ordered heart is to love the right thing to the right degree in the right way with the right kind of love.*
>
> —Augustine

My high school had one of the best gymnastic teams in the state. I had been a part of both a state champion and a runner-up team. Individually, I was getting better every year; I had made the all-state team and our city newspaper's "Best of the Best" team. I knew my junior year would be the best one yet.

That season started off incredibly. Our team was winning, I was winning, and I was undefeated on my best event, the balance beam. Going into the state championship, I knew I would be able to take home the beam title. I was ready, and the only girls who could give me any competition hadn't qualified to compete.

The Monday before the state championship, I was doing a skill on the beam that I had done hundreds of times without any problem, but for some reason this time, I caught my foot between two landing mats and broke my ankle. As I lay there on the ground, watching my ankle swell to the size of a softball, it seemed everything I had been working for was over. Instead of being able to compete at the meet, I was stuck in a hospital room, recovering from surgery.

Everything I had invested in crumbled apart. I had been counting on this moment—I had trained hard and given my heart to this event, and suddenly my hopes were gone. I tried my best to support and encourage my team anyway, but deep down I was filled with envy that my teammates could compete and I couldn't.

At first, I was very angry with God. It seemed unfair that my dream should be taken away. But in being angry with God, I also began to grow closer to Him, realizing that there must be some reason I was going through this ordeal. I knew that my heart wasn't focused on God; that was why I felt distant from Him. It took my accident to remind me that I do desire a relationship with God, so I started to spend more time every day in prayer, thanking God for the gifts I had been given. I was also reminded that Christ suffered more on the cross to save me than I ever would with a broken ankle. I began to rely on God for strength and patience to learn to walk and eventually do gymnastics again.

> *Only within community is the possibility of knowing and being known, loving and being loved, serving and being served, and celebrating and being celebrated.*
>
> —Gilbert Bilezikian

I strove to give God my best, not only whatever was leftover with my time and energy. I wanted God, not gymnastics, to control my life. I reprioritized my life and got involved in a campus ministry and a small group through my youth ministry. My small group at church sustained me through this time of frustration, anger, and physical recovery. I now have friends who share my faith; they help me stay committed to God first and then gymnastics.

It took my accident for me to refocus on God and church. God taught me that nothing in my life is more important than my relationship with Him and my commitment to remain in the church community; while sports might not always be there, He always will. God has given me gymnastic skills so I can honor Him through my sports. My first priority needs to be Him, and I have found that my small group is what keeps me focused on Him.

What I Learned

- I need to follow the path God laid for me, not the path I have laid for myself.

- I have to balance my sports life and my church life. They are both important to me, and God gave me both.
- A small group of Christian friends is the most effective way for me to grow in Christ and balance my priorities.
- Sometimes I didn't get what I wanted in sports. I have to remember that God is in control of my life. He has given me athletic abilities for a reason, and He wants me to enjoy that.

Questions for Reflection or Discussion

1. Matthew 6:33 says, "'But seek first the kingdom of God and His righteousness, and all these things will be provided for you.'" What does this verse tell you about prioritizing God, church, and sports?

2. Do you feel you have put God and the church on the shelf? What will it take to change this?

3. What plans do you need to give up right now so you can better follow God? What do you think God would do with your athletic abilities if you gave up your own plans?

4. Knowing the need for a small group of friends, like Erin's, who meet on a regular basis and supports you, challenges you, and keeps you focused on God, what can you do to make sure you're in one of these groups? How can you get involved in this type of environment?

Excellence IN ACTION

PAUL: *Persecutor to Proclaimer*

| **Acts 9:1–30** | Paul grew up climbing the ladder in his religious society and would have been considered a Pharisee, a strict observer of the laws of faith. |

Most of the leaders of Jewish religious society didn't believe Christ was who He said He was. Paul stood by approvingly as an angry mob took Stephen, one of Jesus' followers, and stoned him to death. On the authority of the chief priests, Paul himself put many of Jesus' followers in prison, and when they were facing a death sentence, he cast his vote against them. Many times he went from town to town and from one place of worship to another to have them punished.

On one occasion, Paul and a band of men had permission from the chief priests in Jerusalem to go to Damascus and take prisoner any member of the group who followed Jesus. As he approached Damascus, a bright light from heaven flashed around him, knocking him to the ground. He heard a voice say to him, "Why do you persecute Me?" Paul asked who was speaking to him, and was told, "Jesus, the One you are trying to destroy." Paul got up, opened his eyes, and discovered he couldn't see. So he decided to follow Jesus' instructions; he went into the city and waited for someone to tell him what to do.

After Paul's stunning encounter with Jesus, he waited three days in Damascus, fasting and praying. Then Ananias, a follower of Jesus, came to the house and laid his hands on Paul. He told Paul that Jesus had sent him so that Paul might see again and follow Christ. Paul's sight was restored! He got up and was baptized as a follower of Jesus.

After several days with the disciples in Damascus, Paul—a former bounty hunter who had condemned those who proclaimed Jesus' message—went to the synagogues, proclaiming that Jesus was the Son of God.

Paul was misguided in his efforts to please God, and God let him know by giving him a wake-up call. He repented of his life of legalism—seeing God as a harsh judge demanding extremely rigid behavior—and helped people accept God's love and forgiveness.

Later, Paul wrote a lot of the New Testament, while he lived a courageous life for the sake of the church. Despite hardships, beatings, and jailings, Paul obeyed God, and God used him in a mighty way to build the church.

Questions for Reflection or Discussion

1. How would you feel if you suddenly discovered what you had fought for and staked your life on was wrong? How long would it take for you to recover?

2. Who in your life has helped you understand the truth about Jesus? What was your wake-up call like?

3. Paul obeyed God and God used him in a mighty way. What kept Paul going? What keeps you going? How can God use you in a mighty way to build the church?

DECISIONS

JOHN

Sports and involvement in my youth ministry make my schedule pretty busy. I often have hard choices about what I can commit to. One of my hardest choices over the years was choosing between summer football camp and my youth ministry's summer missions trip. For three summers, I chose the missions trip over football camp. It was a hard decision, but it was a crucial time for developing my faith, and I wanted to be there. I know I missed a great time at football camp, but I never regretted my decisions.

> *God wants us to be people, not robots, and that means we must make decisions.*
>
> —John Ortberg

In the beginning stages of my football career, missing summer camp didn't hurt my chances of being a part of the team. But the summer before my senior year was a different story. I had really improved as a player and was the team's number-one running back. The coaches expected me to set an example by attending summer football camp. The decision was harder than ever before. My church leaders wanted me to go on the missions trip, and my coaches and teammates were counting on me being at football camp. The pressure was mounting, and I didn't know which way to go. I wanted to do both!

> *"Your heart must not be troubled. Believe in God; believe also in Me."*
>
> —Jesus
> John 14:1

I had always been taught that no matter what, all church activities came before sports. Because the missions trip was to help others, I figured God would want me to do that. I prayed about it and tried to make a decision, but God was not giving me clear answers. I felt guilty that I even wanted to go to football camp, as if maybe even considering it made me a bad Christian. I wanted to be a leader on my team that year and set an example for others, and summer camp would start the year off on the right foot.

I realized that serving God with my whole heart doesn't mean I have to always choose church activities. Both summer camp and the missions trip were good options for me. God wants me in a relationship with Him and others, and He will direct me to the activity that will make the most Kingdom impact.

A few weeks into the summer, my youth minister found out that the summer missions trip would be moved up three weeks. Now it didn't interfere with football camp! I was so excited to see how God had answered my prayers. I know this won't happen every time, but I'm thankful that God orchestrated it so that I could go to both. I know that most times I will have to make a hard choice.

God has distinct plans for us—those plans sometimes include church events and sometimes school activities. God made my decision easy for me, this time, but also taught me that I can trust Him in the future as well.

What I Learned

- When I make decisions that involve conflicting church and nonchurch events, I need to ask God for direction and answers and have faith to follow God's leading.
- God will let me know where He wants me to be and how I can serve Him. He may be calling me to be at church or at sports and I need to be open to His guidance.
- God is always faithful. When I'm faithful to His leading in my life, He has a way of working things out for me.

Questions for Reflection or Discussion

1. What are some conflicts you have between church and sports right now? Where do you think God is calling you to be? Do you think it's possible that God would direct you away from a church activity?

2. Many of us have too much going on with school, sports, and church to do everything. What do you need to do to make your schedule more balanced and to focus on the right things for you?

3. Is it hard to hear His leading sometimes? Read these Scriptures: "Without guidance, people fall, but with many counselors there is deliverance" (Prov. 11:14) and "Plans fail when there is no counsel, but with many advisers they succeed" (Prov. 15:22). When you're having a hard time making a decision, who do you ask for guidance?

Excellence IN ACTION
PAUL: *One Message, New Ways*

**Acts
17:16–34**

Paul's ministry involved traveling from city to city, proclaiming Jesus as Messiah and establishing local churches. Many people believed the message, and the church was growing rapidly. After a successful visit to Berea, Paul decided to go to Athens and spread his message to the people there.

Paul and his companions had to be feeling good as they journeyed to Athens. For all practical purposes; they had just hit a home run for the kingdom of God in Berea. Most people walking down that road to Athens would think, *Let's go do it the same way in Athens as we did in Berea,* but not Paul.

He knew the message of God's love and forgiveness was the same everywhere. But people everywhere are different, so Paul went around Athens and observed what made these people tick. He saw their many statues and temples to the gods. They even had a statue that read, "To an unknown God." Paul discovered that Athens was an idea place; people liked to hear about, and talk about, the latest ideas. So Paul talked openly about Jesus with people in the marketplace and the synagogues. Some people were curious to hear more about these new ideas, so Paul was invited to the Areopagus, a place where the best and brightest gathered for discussion.

When Paul addressed the crowd at the Areopagus, he said, "Men of Athens, I see that in every way you are very religious. For as I walked around and looked carefully at your objects of worship, I even found an altar with the inscription: 'To an unknown God.'

Now what you worship as unknown, I am going to proclaim to you." Paul went on to tell them about God, and even among a tough audience some believed Paul's message that day.

Paul connected with the people of Athens, and in turn they were able to connect with God. He had discovered what made the people of Athens tick, and he used what they knew as truth to connect them with the everlasting truth of Jesus.

Questions for Reflection or Discussion

1. There is one message and an endless variety of ways to share it. How can you learn to know the people with whom you want to share your faith? How will that affect the way you present the message of Christ?

2. What are you doing, personally and in your church, to proclaim the one true message? How can you do this more effectively?

3. When you know people believe differently from you, are you tempted to treat them as opponents or friends? Paul began talking to the people of Athens by congratulating them on their religious enthusiasm, even though he believed very differently about God. Why do you think Paul did that? What people in your life need to be treated as friends rather than opponents?

A NEW DEFINITION OF WINNING

KAI

I have always been involved both in athletics and in church. I have played baseball for years and have been attending church with my family since I was born! For a long time I didn't see how my sports and church life related to one another. Once I started high school, though, God began to show me how the competitiveness I developed playing baseball could transfer to my youth ministry. I wanted to incorporate my sports life—including my teammates—with my church life, so I decided to start a sports program for my youth ministry.

It was easy for me to invite my teammates to church for a basketball game, and once they were there, they were open to hear a message being delivered that night. One of my teammates told me that at our youth group was the first time he fit in at a church. He had always thought church kids were weird and weak, but he now saw something different. My youth minister encouraged me to continue to use my competitive spirit and leadership qualities to get other students involved.

Set your minds on what is above, not on what is on the earth.

—Colossians 3:2

While it was easy for me to relate with other athletes, it was more of a struggle getting students outside of sports involved. I sometimes got frustrated because having nonathletes involved meant taking the intensity level of our competition down a notch. God had to humble me and show me that getting other students involved in church and comfortable in our youth ministry was more important than winning a pickup game. My definition of winning changed from winning the game to winning the person.

God made me with a competitive nature that makes an impact on the playing field. I can use the same behavior in ministry at church. I have to be myself, so I've learned to get fired up about making my youth group a great place for my non-Christian friends. I've learned to encourage new players instead of getting frustrated when we aren't winning. By encouraging others and keeping the competition in perspective, I build relationships that allow me to share Christ. Sports ministry at my church is a great opportunity for God to use me, and by allowing God to mold my competitive nature, I've been able to make an impact on my campus.

What I Learned

- I can use how God wired me to build up the church.
- Some people are different from me—not everyone is as competitive and intense. I need to keep myself in check when we're playing together and focus on making other people feel welcome and building relationships with them.

Christ does not speak about recognizing our neighbor but about being a neighbor.

—Søren Kierkegaard

- I need to keep a mind-set of encouragement, not frustration. God wants me to enjoy church activities, but the ultimate goal is to see people come to know Him and grow in Him, not only to win a game.

Questions for Reflection or Discussion

1. Describe a time you let your competitive spirit go too far. How were other people harmed in the process?
2. How could you use your passion for sports to help your ministry at church? How could your youth group welcome your teammates? What are the steps that you might take to see this happen in your church?
3. Read Galatians 5:13–15. What do these verses tell you about being overly competitive? How can you remember to love others as yourself?

Excellence IN ACTION

PAUL: *Champion for the Church*

2 Timothy 4

The apostle Paul's intensity was unmatched regarding the church and advancing the cause of Christ in the world. He had a passion for the church that marked all of his actions and writings. He considered his life not worth much if he was not achieving the mission he was handed from the Lord.

Paul was very strategic: Most of his ventures focused on key cities, where many different types of people lived. The message of Christ was heard and then taken all over the world from those places.

When a church was starting, Paul stayed to guide its growth. He developed deep relationships, like the ones with the elders in Ephesus, whom he treasured and on future journeys would revisit. He knew he couldn't do his work alone, so he invested time in teaching other men to carry on the work he started—men like Titus, Timothy, and Silas.

Paul was not a superhero; he was just a man who lived fully devoted to God. He endured much and suffered for his calling. He spoke in front of many high-ranking officials, scholars, and even kings. In front of King Agrippa he told his story, and when the king asked if Paul was trying to persuade him to be a Christian, Paul quickly replied, "I pray that not only you but all who are listening to me today may become what I am." He also passionately challenged others to stand firm, hold on to the faith, and finish the race before them.

Paul chose Timothy as one of the people who would continue his work. In 2 Timothy 4 are some of the last words Paul wrote, guidelines for what would be required of Timothy as he continued Paul's work: "But as for you, keep a clear head about everything, endure hardship, do the work of an evangelist, fulfill your ministry" (v. 5).

He then summed up his life of following Jesus, and his passion and pursuit of the church, in the form of a challenge for Timothy to follow him: "I have fought the good fight, I have finished the race, I have kept the faith. In the future, there is reserved for me the crown of righteousness, which the Lord, the righteous Judge, will give me on that day, and not only to me, but to all those who have loved His appearing" (vv. 7–8). What a way to end! Imagine what it would feel like to be able to say those words as the apostle Paul did or hear those words as Timothy did and be encouraged to fight, to finish, to keep the faith. The once-misguided Pharisee Saul ended as the apostle Paul, champion for the church.

Questions for Reflection or Discussion

1. Paul had a dream for the church and he was willing to sacrifice everything for it. What is your dream for the church? What role do you think God wants you to play in that dream?
2. When are you tempted to give up on what God has called you to? How do you overcome hard times and difficult relationships?
3. Whom could you encourage or mentor to become a champion of the church? How would you invest in that person?

THE COMMUNITY OF THE CHURCH

DAVID

My excitement preparing for my first full week of college was immeasurable. I had just received a scholarship to play baseball at my dream college. Things couldn't have been better. I headed off to college, ready to live my own life and excited about making my own rules, not living by my parents' rules.

I had been involved with Fellowship of Christian Athletes in high school, and I wanted to be part of a ministry in college. I got involved in Campus Outreach, but baseball season was quickly approaching, and I didn't have time for everything. Trying to get into shape and be ready for the season began to take its toll on me, and nothing was going to stop me from starting as freshman.

One day as I was walking down a flight of stairs, I tripped and went tumbling. Halfway down, I felt a pop in my right knee. I knew at that moment it was serious. Later that day at the doctor's, I found out I had torn cartilage in my knee. Then I heard the worst three words an athlete could possibly hear: "You need surgery."

> God has willed that we should seek and find His living Word in the witness of a brother. . . . Therefore, the Christian needs another Christian who speaks God's Word to him.
>
> —Dietrich Bonhoeffer

I was devastated. I had to sit out the whole season, and my coach told me I was going to lose my scholarship because of the injury. I began to question God and His plan. I had planned on sharing the gospel with all my teammates, starting a Bible study on the team, and serving God through baseball. I couldn't imagine God taking that from me, but God began to show me that my plan was not necessarily His.

A few months went by, and I continued to question my faith and doubt God's plan. I was frustrated and discouraged but wanted to see God in this. I went to a local church and got involved in a small group. Through this group, I met a leader who really shared his life with me. He took time out to care for me when I needed it the most. The love and acceptance I received during this time was exactly what I needed to get back on track with God.

My small-group leader also shared with me the importance of being involved with a church and how crucial it was for my spiritual growth. I didn't really grasp that concept until he shared a few verses that still ring true in my mind today: "Let us hold on to the confession of our hope without wavering, for He who promised is faithful. And let us be concerned about one another in order to promote love and good works, not staying away from our meetings, as some habitually do, but encouraging each other, and all the more as you see the day drawing near" (Heb. 10:23–25).

Over the months that followed, I realized how important it is for Christians to be a part of a church family in which believers can be challenged and sharpened. I was able to grow and be developed there, in a group that challenged and guided me in my spiritual journey. I was encouraged, equipped, and challenged to be the man God wants me to be. Now I'm leading a group of five student athletes in my church who are taking the gospel to their teammates and schools. Through my experience of having knee surgery, I was able to realize the importance of a church family, one that's there for more than a season or two but throughout my life. The impact my church has had on my life far outweighs the rewards I may have received on the field.

> *Therefore encourage one another and build each other up as you are already doing.*
>
> —1 Thessalonians 5:11

What I Learned

- It isn't enough to rely only on my successes as an athlete. I have to rely on God, Christian friends, and the local church as well.
- Sometimes we need a group of people to help us through a difficult time—it's too hard to make it through alone.
- God desires me to be part of a local church, a spiritual community in which I can grow and be developed over my entire spiritual journey, not through only a season.

Questions for Reflection or Discussion

1. It can be frustrating when you suddenly realize God's plan is not the same as yours. Have you experienced this? How were you able to accept it and understand God's plan?

2. Read Hebrews 10:23–25 again. How do these verses affect you? Where do you find this kind of community?

3. With the big commitment that sports requires, how do you make a spiritual community within the local church a priority?

Sports Outreach Association

is a national and international ministry that exists to
help the local church build effective sports and fitness
ministries by providing vision, resources, and training
to equip and encourage church leaders.

To find out more about Sports Outreach Association
and membership, please visit our Web site at
www.SportsOutreach.us
or contact us at
Sports Outreach Association
435 Pennsylvania Avenue #144
Glen Ellyn, IL 60137
630-205-7152

Get Deep. Get TruthQuest.